IPL AUCTIONS

IPL Auctions

TEAMS, TACTICS, TRIUMPHS UNFOLD

Mack Rafeal

Spectra Enterprise

Contents

Table of Content

Introduction

The Indian Chief Association (IPL), a cricketing spectacle that has caught the creative mind of millions all over the planet, rises above the limits of customary games competitions. While the on-field fights among bat and ball exhibit unmatched expertise and physicality, the off-field show during the IPL barters adds a special aspect to the association. The IPL barters are a display in themselves, a yearly festival where establishments participate in high-stakes offering battles to gather their fantasy groups. These closeouts are the cauldron where methodologies are produced, dreams are traded, and the destiny of groups for the impending season is fixed.

In the terrific auditorium of the IPL barters, each establishment fastidiously makes its procedure to get the administrations of the most sought after players. The groups take part in a fragile difficult exercise, gauging the requirement for star power against the limitations of a financial plan cap. The specialty of exploring and planning becomes vital as groups strive for the marks of marquee players who have the possibility to influence the fortunes of a match without any help. The strategies utilized during the closeouts frequently mirror the bigger vision that establishments harbor for the season ahead. It isn't just about procuring players; about building a strong unit can endure the afflictions of an exhausting competition and arise successful.

The sale table turns into a combat zone where group proprietors, mentors, and experts merge, equipped with information, bits of knowledge, and a smart comprehension of the game. With a proper spending plan available to them, the establishments should explore the intricacies of the bartering room, pursuing key choices that will shape the fate of their group. The appeal of headliners with demonstrated histories conflicts with the realism of distinguishing arising gifts who can be prepared into future stalwarts. This complicated dance of choices makes the IPL barters an arresting scene, mixing the components of procedure, financial matters, and cricketing insight into an exciting blend.

The group sytheses that rise up out of the IPL barters are an impression of the steadily developing elements of the cricketing scene. T20 cricket, with its frantic speed and accentuation on development, requests a special arrangement of abilities from its members. Establishments are not only searching for run-scorers and wicket-takers; they look for players who can adjust to the unique requests of the configuration. The idea of all-rounders acquires unmistakable quality as groups look for players fit for making significant commitments with both bat and ball. Flexibility turns into a valued resource, and establishments scour the ability pool to uncover players who can fill different jobs inside the group.

The bartering table is likewise a phase where longshots can prearrange fantasy stories. Players who could have been disregarded in ordinary configurations wind up popular as groups look for whole jewels that can sparkle brilliantly in the T20 design. The IPL barters have turned into a passage for youthful and moderately obscure players to sling themselves into the spotlight, displaying their abilities on a worldwide stage. The sale room, subsequently, isn't simply a space of laid out stars; it is a commercial center of dreams where ability, regardless of notoriety, can track down its actual worth.

As the sales unfurl, the establishments are not simply gaining players; they are building stories. Each bid, every securing, and each delivery add to the general story of a group's excursion. The maintenance of vital participants is much of the time an essential move to keep up with steadiness and protect the center character of a group. Then again, delivering players can be a cognizant choice to patch up the crew, imbue new blood, and adjust to the changing elements of the game. The accounts are woven around the players as well as around the group ethos, the brand personality, and the desires that the establishment harbors.

The victories in the IPL are not exclusively estimated regarding triumphs on the field; they are likewise checked by the viability of the systems executed during the barterings. The connection between's an effective closeout and on-field achievement is clear, with groups that work out some kind of harmony between star power and group union frequently arising as leaders. The IPL, in its substance, is a competition where the elements of progress are complex - it isn't just about gathering a gathering of capable people yet about producing an aggregate personality that can endure the hardships of a serious season.

The victories, in any case, are not selective to the groups alone. Players, as well, wind up at the cusp of fresh starts and difficulties as they switch loyalties and wear the shades of various establishments. The barterings act as a mixture where players from different foundations, societies, and playing styles unite to make a mosaic of cricketing brightness. The association's worldwide allure is highlighted by the presence of global stars, who carry their own energy and panache to the competition. The IPL, consequently, rises above the limits of identity, transforming cricket into a genuinely worldwide scene.

1. **Overview of the Indian Premier League (IPL)**

The Indian Chief Association (IPL) remains as a paragon of cricketing display, a competition that has reclassified the scene of the game since its beginning in 2008. Arising against the setting of India's blossoming T20 cricket intensity, the IPL quickly developed into a worldwide peculiarity, dazzling fans across mainlands with its powerful blend of super charged cricket, excitement, and fabulousness. As an expert Twenty20 cricket association in India, the IPL isn't only a competition; a wearing fair rises above the limits of traditional cricket, mixing diversion with physicality to make an unmatched survey insight.

At its center, the IPL is an establishment based association, where groups addressing various urban communities and districts fight it out for incomparability. The association was conceptualized by the Leading body of Control for Cricket in India (BCCI) as a reaction to the developing fame of T20 cricket and as a way to imbue new life into the game. What unfolded, be that as it may, outperformed all assumptions, as the IPL arose as a mammoth, inside the cricketing crew as well as in the worldwide donning field.

The construction of the IPL is worked around the T20 design, known for its quick moving and dangerous nature. Each group goes head to head against the others in a cooperative organization during the association stage, with the top-performing groups progressing to the end of the season games. The end of the season games comprise of Qualifier 1, Eliminator, Qualifier 2, and the Last, finishing in the delegated of the IPL champions. This arrangement guarantees that the competition keeps up with its power all through, with each match conveying huge ramifications for the standings and the quest for the sought after prize.

One of the characterizing elements of the IPL is the sale framework through which groups fabricate their crews. The yearly IPL closeout is an exhibition in itself, where establishments take part in vivacious offering battles to get the administrations of players from around the world. The bartering is a microcosm of the association's ethos, consolidating cricketing intuition with monetary reasonability as groups endeavor to figure out some kind of harmony between star power and group union inside the imperatives of a foreordained spending plan cap. The closeout cycle adds an additional layer of show to the association, forming the accounts and procedures that will unfurl on the field in the approaching season.

The worldwide allure of the IPL is elevated by the support of global cricketing symbols. The association fills in as a stage for players from various nations to meet up, encouraging a feeling of kinship and solid rivalry. The mixture of different playing styles and societies makes a lively embroidery of cricket, adding to the widespread charm of the IPL. Worldwide stars, going from prepared campaigners to arising gifts, strive for an opportunity to feature their abilities on this stupendous stage, further improving the competition's worldwide importance.

Past the cricketing activity, the IPL is inseparable from amusement. The association has flawlessly mixed sports and showbiz, with team promoters, music, and amazing functions becoming indispensable parts of the IPL experience. The combination of cricket with diversion has expanded the association's allure, drawing in no-nonsense cricket fans as well as a more extensive crowd that looks for an all encompassing and vivid wearing experience. The IPL has turned into a festival of the soul of cricket, a celebration that enamors the creative mind of millions and rises above the limits of the battleground.

The monetary elements of the IPL are significant, underlining its status as one of the most rewarding cricket associations internationally.

The competition has been an impetus for monetary development in Indian cricket, with the implantation of sponsorships, broadcasting freedoms arrangements, and brand supports raising the financial profile of the taking part establishments. The IPL has given a rewarding stage to cricketers as well as generated a flourishing biological system of organizations, sponsors, and media substances that gain by the association's tremendous ubiquity.

The IPL's example of overcoming adversity isn't without its reasonable portion of discussions and difficulties. Throughout the long term, the association has wrestled with issues, for example, match-fixing embarrassments, player careless activities, and discussions encompassing the booking and organization. Be that as it may, the versatility of the IPL and its capacity to endure these hardships highlights its importance in the cricketing scene. The association has arisen more grounded after every difficulty, supporting status as a juggernaut is digging in for the long haul.

The IPL's effect stretches out past the limits of the cricket field, making a permanent imprint on the game's scene. The association has been a favorable place for youthful gifts, giving a springboard to growing cricketers to grandstand their abilities and leave an imprint on the worldwide stage. The examples of overcoming adversity of players found through the IPL feature the association's part in supporting and advancing cricketing ability.

Notwithstanding its effect on individual professions, the IPL has likewise affected how cricket is played and seen all around the world. The association's accentuation on advancement, animosity, and versatility has saturated the more extensive cricketing society, impacting systems in different arrangements of the game. The IPL has turned into a pioneer, molding the development of cricket and filling in as a lab for trial and error and advancement in playing styles.

As the IPL keeps on developing, it faces the test of finding some kind of harmony among custom and advancement. The perfectionists might wail over the coming of T20 cricket and its effect on the old style types of the game, yet there is no rejecting that the IPL has infused another rent of life into the game.

The association remains as a demonstration of cricket's capacity to adjust and rehash itself, taking care of the different preferences of a worldwide crowd while protecting the quintessence of the game.

2. **Significance of IPL Auctions in shaping team dynamics**

The IPL barters, a yearly scene that goes before the cricketing party, are something other than a commercial center for players; they are the cauldron where the fate of groups is manufactured, and the actual embodiment of the association's seriousness is refined.

The meaning of the IPL barters in molding group elements couldn't possibly be more significant, for what it's worth during these high-stakes offering wars that the diagrams for progress are considered, and the stories of wins and difficulties are composed.

At the core of the IPL barters lies the idea of player barters, a novel and riveting cycle where establishments take part in a furious fight to gain the most sought after cricketing ability. The elements of these barterings are molded by a mix of cricketing keenness, key preparation, and monetary judiciousness, as each establishment tries to construct a crew that can explore the exhausting difficulties of the T20 design. The cycle isn't just about gathering a gathering of individual players; about building a strong unit can complete one another qualities and moderate shortcomings.

One of the crucial parts of the IPL barters is the spending plan cap forced on each establishment. This monetary limitation adds a layer of intricacy to the procedures, constraining groups to pursue determined choices inside the bounds of their distributed financial plan. The essential portion of assets turns into a fragile difficult exercise, with establishments looking to get marquee players while likewise guaranteeing they have the profundity and flexibility expected for a requesting competition. The financial plan cap, in this way, goes about as an evening out factor, forestalling the rise of cricketing governments and advancing equality among the groups.

The meaning of the IPL barters is complemented by the way that they mark the start of another part for each establishment. The piece of the crew goes through a transformation as players are purchased, exchanged, or delivered, prompting the development of a group that is a mix of involvement and youth, hostility and artfulness. The closeouts are the material where the group's character is painted, and the choices made during this interaction resound all through the season, impacting the group's fortunes on the field.

Procedures utilized during the barterings frequently mirror the more extensive vision that establishments have for the season. A few groups focus on star influence, going a little overboard on laid out players who carry with them an abundance of involvement and a demonstrated history. Others pick a more sober minded approach, putting resources into arising gifts and potential match-champs who might not have gathered a similar degree of acknowledgment. The variety in approaches adds interest to the barterings, as groups cut out unmistakable ways to progress, each established in its own arrangement of methods of reasoning and needs.

The meaning of the IPL barters is highlighted by their job in cultivating a dynamic and serious player market. The offering wars decide the destiny of players as well as lay out their reasonable worth, with effective exhibitions in past releases frequently converting into higher offers.

The closeouts, thusly, become a phase where players can lift their vocations, secure monetary dependability, and earn worldwide respect. For youthful and arising gifts, the IPL barters address a passage to the global stage, giving a stage to exhibit their abilities on a fabulous scale.

The closeout elements likewise assume a critical part in reshaping group competitions and unions. Players who were once colleagues might end up on inverse sides of the war zone, adding an additional layer of show and force to the on-field challenges. The sales, in this way, add to the account of the association, making subplots and storylines that add profundity to the general show of the IPL.

The group elements that rise out of the IPL barters are not static; they are dependent upon ceaseless assessment and transformation. Halfway through the season, establishments have the chance to reconsider their crews and attachment any holes that might have arisen. The mid-season move window permits players to move between groups, giving a component to establishments to address explicit requirements or reinforce their crews in view of the developing elements of the competition. This adaptability guarantees that the groups stay dynamic substances, equipped for adjusting to the difficulties presented by wounds, structure droops, or changing key necessities.

The meaning of the IPL barters stretches out past the limits of the battleground; it saturates the whole environment of the association. The closeouts are a wellspring of expectation and energy for fans, who enthusiastically anticipate the revealing of their group's new signings and the procedures utilized by the administration. The sales likewise act as a stage for brands and backers to conform to the association, utilizing the star power and worldwide allure of the players in question. The monetary consequences of the closeouts are significant, with player contracts, sponsorship arrangements, and broadcasting freedoms adding to the monetary juggernaut that is the IPL.

The group elements formed by the IPL barters are not just about gathering a gathering of cricketers; they are tied in with building a brand. Each establishment addresses an extraordinary character, with its tones, logos, and group culture adding to the bigger story of the association. The progress of an establishment isn't exclusively estimated in that frame of mind on-field wins; it is likewise measured by the reverberation it makes among fans, the brand faithfulness it develops, and the persevering through heritage it lays out. The barterings, in this way, assume a crucial part in deciding the wearing outcome of a group as well as its business suitability and social importance.

As the association develops, the meaning of the IPL barters is probably going to escalate. The rising globalization of cricket, combined with the growing ability pool, guarantees that the sales will stay a dynamic and wildly challenged field.

Establishments will keep on refining their techniques, utilizing information examination, exploring networks, and cricketing aptitude to uncover jewels and make winning blends. The barterings will keep on being a gauge of cricketing patterns, mirroring the developing needs and inclinations of groups in the consistently changing scene of T20 cricket.

3. **Brief history of IPL Auctions and their evolution**

The Indian Chief Association (IPL) barters, an exciting scene that goes before each time of the T20 spectacle, have a captivating history set apart by development and development. Since its beginning in 2008, the closeouts have developed from a speculative trial into a refined and high-stakes issue, molding the elements of group organization and systems. The excursion of IPL barters is a demonstration of the association's capacity to adjust to changing cricketing scenes and to consistently rethink the boundaries of sports barters.

The idea of player barters in the IPL was imagined to infuse a component of energy and unconventionality into group building processes. The main sale, held in Mumbai in February 2008, was a spearheading work to lay out another worldview in cricket organization. Establishment proprietors, group authorities, and players assembled at the Hilton Pinnacles to observe a noteworthy occasion that would proceed to upset the financial matters and elements of cricket.

In the debut closeout, 77 players went under the sledge, with each establishment furnished with a financial plan of $5 million. The configuration was a blend of shut and open offering, adding a quality of tension to the procedures. The spotlight was on laid out global stars as well as on unheralded homegrown players who tried to leave an imprint on the fantastic stage. Shane Warne, then at the sundown of his famous lifetime, arose as the marquee player, being purchased by the Rajasthan Royals for an amount of $450,000.

The underlying sell-offs set the vibe for the years to come, laying out the IPL as a cricketing festival where procedures were conceived, and vocations were changed. The sales turned into a yearly custom, enthusiastically anticipated by fans and partners the same, as groups participated in vivacious offering battles to get the administrations of their ideal players. The arrangement advanced, consolidating developments, for example, the Option to Match (RTM) card, which permitted establishments to hold explicit players by matching the most noteworthy bid they got in the closeout.

The advancement of IPL sell-offs can be followed through the changing elements of player valuations. In the early years, the accentuation was on obtaining star power, with global players ordering over the top totals.

Any semblance of Kevin Pietersen, Andrew Flintoff, and MS Dhoni were among the high-profile acquisitions, getting record-breaking sums in the barterings. The interest for marquee players made a swelled market, with establishments frequently going overboard on a couple of key people while filling their other crews with moderately less popular players.

As the association developed, a change in system became clear. Groups began perceiving the benefit of building adjusted crews, zeroing in the collaboration of the group as opposed to depending exclusively on individual brightness. The development of homegrown gifts like Ravindra Jadeja, R Ashwin, and Jasprit Bumrah exhibited the significance of supporting neighborhood ability, and establishments started putting all the more sensibly in the homegrown player pool. The pattern mirrored a more extensive change in the cricketing scene, with the spotlight progressively turning towards the T20 design and the worldwide expansion of T20 associations.

The mid-2010s saw a change in perspective in the design of the closeouts with the presentation of the maintenance strategy. This permitted establishments to hold a specific number of players in front of the closeout, giving dependability to group pieces and guaranteeing the congruity of vital participants. The maintenance strategy additionally achieved the idea of 'pre-closeout exchanging,' permitting groups to exchange players among themselves before the conventional sale process initiated. These progressions added vital layers to the group building process, empowering establishments to purposely shape their crews more.

The year 2018 denoted one more critical development with the acquaintance of the Right with Match (RTM) card. This element permitted groups to hold a player by matching the most noteworthy bid they got for the expressed player in the bartering. The RTM card infused a component of strategic moving, as establishments needed to choose whether to utilize their card in a calculated manner or let a player go and afterward bid for them in the open sale. The RTM card modified the elements of the barterings, making them more unpredictable and key.

The developing accentuation on examination and information driven dynamic additionally impacted the advancement of IPL barters. Establishments started utilizing measurable bits of knowledge, player execution measurements, and exploring reports to distinguish underestimated players and potential match-victors. The combination of cricketing keenness with information science carried another aspect to the closeouts, empowering groups to pursue more educated and vital decisions.

The bartering elements additionally reflected the changing scene of worldwide cricket, with players progressively focusing on T20 associations like the IPL over conventional organizations. The monetary charm of the association, combined with the openness it presented on a worldwide stage, made it an alluring suggestion for players from all cricketing countries.

The cosmopolitan idea of the IPL, with groups including a blend of Indian and global stars, added to the association's general allure.

The IPL barters, by their actual nature, are an impression of the financial elements of cricket. The association's capacity to draw in high-profile supports, secure worthwhile telecom bargains, and create income through ticket deals and product plays had a critical impact in molding the monetary scene of the game. The player barters, with their eye-getting offers and extravagant agreements, have turned into an image of the monetary ability of the IPL and its effect on the more extensive cricketing environment.

As the IPL barters keep on advancing, they face continuous difficulties and discussions. The unevenness in player pay rates, with a couple of marquee players procuring essentially more than their partners, has started conversations about the compensation cap and income sharing models. The association additionally wrestles with the sensitive harmony between business contemplations and cricketing ethos, with worries about player responsibility and burnout in the period of persevering T20 cricket.

Looking forward, the eventual fate of IPL barters guarantees further advancement and variation. The association is probably going to investigate roads for upgraded fan commitment during the sales, utilizing computerized stages and intelligent encounters to interface with a worldwide crowd. The coming of new innovations, like computer generated simulation and expanded reality, may additionally change how closeouts are led, giving a more vivid and dynamic experience for fans.

Chapter 1

The Auction Arena

The Closeout Field of the Indian Chief Association (IPL) remains as a stadium where cricketing fates are formed, unions are fashioned, and methodologies are revealed. This powerful commercial center, where establishments participate in high-stakes offering battles to secure the administrations of players, is an exhibition that rises above the limits of game, mixing show, procedure, and monetary judiciousness into an exciting mixture. As the substance of the association, the Sale Field isn't just a conditional space; it is the landmark where the stories of win and misfortune, of dreams traded, unfurl.

The Sale Field's commencement in 2008 denoted a change in perspective in the manner cricket was coordinated and consumed. In a takeoff from traditional player enrollment techniques, the IPL presented the idea of sell-offs, changing the group incorporating process into an arresting scene. The debut closeout was a notable occasion, held at the Hilton Pinnacles in Mumbai, where establishments, outfitted with foreordained financial plans, a participated in an unfamiliar area of shut and open offering to collect their crews.

The marquee players in the primary sale included cricketing illuminating presences like Shane Warne, MS Dhoni, and Ricky Ponting.

The meaning of the Sale Field was quickly obvious as the offering wars unfurled, with the Rajasthan Royals getting the administrations of Warne for $450,000. The sale design, with its mix of mystery and vain behaviors, added a layer of interest to the procedures, raising the player securing interaction to a dramatic presentation that reverberated with fans and partners the same.

Throughout the long term, the Closeout Field has gone through a captivating development, reflecting the changing elements of cricket and the actual association. The presentation of the maintenance strategy, permitting establishments to hold a specific number of players before the closeout, carried another aspect to the group building process. This strategy gave soundness to group sytheses as well as added an essential layer as establishments needed to reasonably choose which players to hold and which to deliver into the sale pool.

The Option to Match (RTM) card, presented in 2018, further elevated the essential complexities of the Sale Field. This card permitted establishments to hold a player by matching the most noteworthy bid they got for the expressed player in the bartering. The RTM card infused a component of tension and strategic moving, as groups needed to choose when to play their cards in a calculated manner and when to allow a player to go out from the shadows sell off. The developing standards and advancements have transformed the Closeout Field into a cerebral war zone where cricketing intuition, monetary computations, and key prescience impact.

The elements of the Bartering Field are unpredictably attached to the monetary goals of the IPL. The association's monetary model, with its income streams from broadcasting privileges, sponsorships, and establishment proprietorship, straight-forwardly influences the financial aspects of the barterings. The spending plans distributed to establishments direct the boundaries inside which they should work, convincing them to settle on wise choices and find some kind of harmony between star power and crew profundity.

The marquee players, frequently worldwide cricketing symbols, become the central places of the Closeout Field. The intense offering battles for these stars are a sign of the association's worldwide allure and monetary clout. The Sale Field is where establishments strive for the mark of players who have cricketing ability as well as the star ability to draw in crowds, supporters, and media consideration. The monetary a lot is on the line, and the Sale Field turns into a milestone where monetary reasonability meets the quest for brilliance.

The Closeout Field isn't just about obtaining players; it is tied in with building accounts. Each bid, every procurement, and each delivery add to the general story of a group's excursion. The maintenance of central members is in many cases an essential move to keep up with security and save the center character of a group.

Then again, delivering players can be a cognizant choice to redo the crew, imbue new blood, and adjust to the changing elements of the game. The accounts are woven around the players as well as around the group ethos, the brand personality, and the yearnings that the establishment harbors.

The essential arranging that unfurls in the Closeout Field is a demonstration of the multifaceted dance between cricketing mastery and monetary keenness. Establishment proprietors, mentors, and experts merge at the closeout table equipped with information, bits of knowledge, and a wise comprehension of the game. The group elements are not just formed by the ability of individual players however by the collaborations and mixes that establishments carefully make during the sale. The effective groups are the ones that explore the intricacies of the Closeout Field with artfulness, settling on essential choices that line up with their vision for the season.

The meaning of the Closeout Field reaches out past the limits of the battleground; it is a phase where longshots can prearrange fantasy stories. Players who could have been ignored in regular configurations end up sought after as groups look for whole precious stones that can sparkle splendidly in the T20 design. The IPL barters have turned into an entryway for youthful and moderately obscure players to launch themselves into the spotlight, displaying their abilities on a worldwide stage. The sale room, thusly, isn't simply a space of laid out stars; it is a commercial center of dreams where ability, independent of notoriety, can track down its actual worth.

The cosmopolitan idea of the IPL, with establishments addressing various urban communities and districts, adds a global flavor to the Closeout Field. The presence of cricketing stars from different nations transforms the closeout into a worldwide commercial center, where players from various cricketing societies unite. The Closeout Field is a mixture of ability, a space where ethnicities break down into the normal quest for progress in the T20 design. The association's worldwide allure is highlighted by the cooperation of global stars, who carry their own pizazz and panache to the competition.

The Bartering Field is likewise an impression of the consistently developing elements of T20 cricket. The configuration, with its accentuation on development, hostility, and versatility, requests a remarkable arrangement of abilities from its members. The idea of all-rounders acquires conspicuousness as groups look for players who can make effective commitments with both bat and ball. Flexibility turns into a valued resource, and establishments scour the ability pool to uncover players who can fill numerous jobs inside the group. The Bartering Field turns into a phase where players are esteemed for their essential abilities as well as for their capacity to contribute across various features of the game.

The monetary components of the Bartering Field are significant, underlining its status as one of the most rewarding cricket barters worldwide.

The association's monetary effect stretches out past the bartering room, with player agreements, sponsorships, and broadcasting privileges adding to the monetary juggernaut that is the IPL. The Closeout Field isn't simply a commercial center for players; it is a stage for brands, publicists, and media elements to fall in line with the association's worldwide allure and contact a huge and various crowd.

1.1 Setting the stage: Venue and atmosphere

Making way for the Indian Head Association (IPL) is a fabulous creation that goes past the limit ropes, including the decision of scene and the energetic climate that pervades each match. The IPL, significantly more than a cricket competition, has secured itself as a social peculiarity, and the determination of settings assumes an essential part in forming the story of this cricketing spectacle. Every arena turns into a theater where the show of T20 cricket unfurls, and the climate turns into the soul that powers the energy of fans and lifts the exhibition to an exceptional level.

The choice of scenes for the IPL is a cautiously organized process, taking into account the calculated viewpoints as well as the verifiable importance and the potential for making a spellbinding feeling. From the notable Eden Nurseries in Kolkata to the Wankhede Arena in Mumbai, every scene conveys its own heritage and adds to the embroidery of the association. The variety in settings reflects the skillet Indian allure of the IPL, transforming it into a celebration that resounds with fans across various districts.

The selection of scenes isn't only a calculated choice; it is an essential move to boost fan commitment and make an electric air. The arenas are chosen in view of their ability, offices, and the cricketing society of the district. Bigger arenas, similar to the M. Chinnaswamy Arena in Bangalore or the Feroz Shah Kotla Ground in Delhi, become the focal point of excited cheers and thunders as fans fill the stands, making an emanation that enhances the power of the matches.

The Wankhede Arena in Mumbai, arranged by the Bedouin Ocean, is a cricketing church that embodies the soul of the city. It has been observer to probably the most notable crossroads in IPL history, and its nearness to the Bollywood entertainment world adds a layer of style to the matches. The thundering ocean of blue — the Mumbai Indians' dedicated fanbase — transforms the Wankhede into a stronghold, with the rowdy cheers reverberating through the stands and resounding across the city.

On the opposite side of the country, the Eden Nurseries in Kolkata remains as a stadium where cricket is a religion, and the Kolkata Knight Riders are the divinities. The sheer size of the arena, equipped for obliging more than 60,000 observers, changes it into a cauldron of feelings.

The waving ocean of purple and gold, the group shades of the Knight Riders, and the serenades of "Korbo Lorbo Jeetbo" (We will do, battle, win) make an air that is both threatening for rivals and thrilling for the host group.

Past the clamoring cities, the IPL stretches out its span to more modest urban communities and towns, carrying the cricketing amusement park to assorted corners of the country. Settings like the Sawai Mansingh Arena in Jaipur and the Holkar Cricket Arena in Indore imbue the association with a local flavor, offering fans in these urban communities an opportunity to encounter the excitement of top-level T20 cricket in their own terrace.

The environment in every scene is additionally uplifted by the presence of energetic and vocal fanbases. The IPL has excelled at transforming cricket matches into diversion displays, and the fans assume a focal part in this change. The association has turned into a blend of societies, with fans from various locales, foundations, and age bunches uniting to make a dynamic mosaic of help for their groups.

The fan commitment goes past the conventional limits of cricket. The IPL has presented components like team promoters, group hymns, and creative in-arena exercises that add to the fair like air. The team promoters, with their high-energy schedules, add to the visual display, while the group hymns become revitalizing cries that join the fans in an ensemble of help. The in-arena exercises, from monster screens catching fan responses to intuitive games and challenges, guarantee that the crowd stays connected all through the match, regardless of the on-field activity.

The IPL has likewise embraced innovation to improve the in-arena experience. Goliath screens show player insights, moment replays, and intelligent surveys, giving fans a far reaching and vivid perspective on the game. The incorporation of innovation reaches out to online entertainment, with hashtags, tweets, and fan collaborations turning into an indispensable piece of the IPL experience. The association has effectively utilized web-based entertainment stages to enhance its range, transforming fans into dynamic members in the bigger story.

The "IPL buzz" isn't restricted to the arenas alone; it saturates the wireless transmissions and computerized spaces, making a virtual climate that reaches out past geological limits. The telecom of matches to a worldwide crowd, combined with the multilingual editorial, changes the IPL into a worldwide exhibition. Whether it's a fan in Chennai, London, or Melbourne, the common experience of the IPL turns into a binding together power that rises above social and geographic partitions.

The IPL's outcome in making a spellbinding environment is likewise credited to the competition's booking. Matches are much of the time played at night, exploiting the cooler temperatures and furnishing fans with an ideal setting to partake in the cricketing activity. The dusk and night games add to the visual scene, with floodlights enlightening the arenas and making an entrancing background for the players to feature their abilities.

The end of the season games and the great last of the IPL are frequently held at unbiased scenes, enhancing the feeling of event and raising the air to a crescendo. These matches become the zenith of long stretches of cricketing show, and the nonpartisan scenes guarantee that the best groups fight it out on fair terms. The nonpartisan settings, whether it's the M. A. Chidambaram Arena in Chennai or the Rajiv Gandhi Global Cricket Arena in Hyderabad, become the material for the great finale, where champions are delegated in the midst of an ensemble of cheers and festivities.

The setting of the IPL goes past the cricketing activity; it stretches out to the energetic urban areas and the different societies that have the matches. The association has turned into a social celebration, with the matchday experience going past the limits of the arena. The group shirts, banners, and pennants decorate the roads, and neighborhood organizations benefit from the cricketing intensity by offering extraordinary advancements and occasions. The IPL turns into a festival that joins networks, encouraging a deep satisfaction and personality for fans who rally behind their neighborhood establishments.

While the IPL has become inseparable from glamour and charm, it likewise embraces a social reason through drives like "Green Games" that advance maintainability and ecological mindfulness. The association has perceived its liability as a significant game and has done whatever it may take to limit its natural impression. The greening of arenas, squander the executives projects, and endeavors to advance eco-accommodating practices add to the association's more extensive effect past the cricket field.

1.2 Auction dynamics and rules

The Indian Chief Association (IPL) barters are an arresting performance center of cricketing show, where groups decisively bid for players in a high-stakes fight for ability. The sale elements and rules, complicatedly intended to adjust rivalry and equality, are a basic part of the association's prosperity. From the mechanics of player offering to the monetary imperatives forced on establishments, the principles of the IPL barters shape the stories, techniques, and results of the competition, adding a layer of intricacy and energy to the player procurement process.

The closeout elements get going as establishments collect at the bartering table, furnished with painstakingly determined methodologies and predefined financial plans.

The interaction is a combination of monetary judiciousness and cricketing keenness, where group proprietors, mentors, and examiners team up to construct a crew that can explore the difficulties of T20 cricket. The stage is set for a scene where the destiny of players remains in a, not entirely set in stone by the essential moves of establishment delegates.

One of the characterizing highlights of the IPL barters is the idea of a compensation cap, a monetary requirement that adds a component of system and reasonableness to the player obtaining process. Each establishment is distributed a foreordained spending plan, and they should work inside the limits of this financial plan while building their crew. The compensation cap forestalls the rise of cricketing governments, guaranteeing that establishments, independent of their monetary muscle, should settle on sensible choices to shape a cutthroat group.

The compensation cap framework likewise presents a feeling of monetary discipline, convincing establishments to carefully designate their assets. Groups should find some kind of harmony between marquee players, who frequently order more significant compensations, and arising abilities or utility players who might offer more prominent incentive for cash. The fragile difficult exercise inside the limitations of the compensation cap mirrors the monetary insight expected to effectively explore the bartering elements.

The player sell off itself is a complex cycle, including different adjusts and stages intended to work with fair offering and vital direction. The barker assumes an essential part in organizing the procedures, establishing a climate that is both extraordinary and dynamic. Players are sorted into various pools in view of their assuming parts and mastery, with each pool addressing a particular range of abilities.

The offering system includes establishments communicating their advantage in a player by raising an oar, flagging their longing to gain the player at the ongoing offering cost. The salesperson then welcomes counter-offers from different establishments, starting a volatile offering war. The cycle go on until just a single establishment stays intrigued, getting the player at the last offered cost. The player is then added to the program of the triumphant establishment.

The Option to Match (RTM) card, presented in 2014, adds a charming layer to the closeout elements. This card permits establishments to hold a specific number of players from their past season's crew by matching the most noteworthy bid they get for those players in the sale. The RTM card infuses a component of tension, as establishments should choose when to play their cards in a calculated manner, guaranteeing they hold central participants without overspending.

The utilization of the RTM card requires cautious thought, as groups should gauge the benefit of holding a player against the chance to procure new ability in the bartering.

The card adds vital intricacy to the sale elements, permitting establishments to keep a level of coherence while likewise mixing new blood into their crews. The RTM card, thusly, turns into a strategic instrument that shapes the general procedure of an establishment during the closeouts.

The uncapped players, frequently youthful and arising gifts, comprise a different pool in the sale elements. Uncapped players are the people who have not addressed their public group in that frame of mind at the hour of the sale. The consideration of this classification gives a stage to less popular players to feature their ability and secure a spot in the rewarding universe of T20 cricket.

The uncapped players frequently become sought-after products in the barterings, with establishments perceiving the potential for uncovering unlikely treasures. The offering battles for uncapped players are described by a blend of intuitions and well balanced plan of action taking, as groups evaluate the players' exhibitions in homegrown and other T20 associations. The examples of overcoming adversity of uncapped players who proceed to make critical commitments feature the dynamic and unusual nature of the sale elements.

The request where players are introduced in the not set in stone by a draw led before the occasion. The randomization guarantees that the bartering elements are not affected by the foreordained request, presenting a component of eccentricism. The draw adds an additional layer of methodology, as establishments should be ready to adjust to the changing scene of accessible players and change their offering anticipates the fly.

The abroad player standard is one more critical part of the bartering elements, with establishments restricted in the quantity of unfamiliar players they can remember for their crew. This limitation highlights the association's accentuation on supporting and displaying neighborhood ability, giving open doors to Indian cricketers to gleam on the worldwide stage. The abroad player openings become top notch resources, and establishments must plan to get a harmony between global star power and homegrown skill.

Vital breaks, one more element acquired from the T20 design, are integrated into the closeout elements. These breaks furnish establishments with a chance to rethink their methodologies, talk with group the board, and recalibrate their offering plans.

The essential breaks add a strategic layer to the closeout, permitting groups to refocus and answer the unfurling elements.

The outcome of the IPL barters is additionally established in the association's hug of innovation and information driven direction. Establishments influence information investigation, exploring organizations, and execution measurements to survey player worth and possible commitments. The utilization of innovation reaches out to the virtual closeout room, where remote offering and ongoing updates guarantee a consistent and productive cycle.

The elements of the IPL barters are not restricted to a solitary occasion; they reach out to mid-season moves and player exchanges. The mid-season move window permits establishments to address holes in their crews by securing players from different groups. This adaptability in group creation adds a powerful component to the association, permitting establishments to adjust to the developing requirements of the competition.

Player exchanges, where groups arrange the trading of players outside the sale window, give an extra road to crews to go through essential changes. The exchange elements permit establishments to upgrade their programs in view of player structure, group necessities, and key contemplations. The exchanges add a component of key prescience, as groups position themselves for progress in the last option phases of the competition.

1.3 Key stakeholders: Franchise owners, coaches, and players

The Indian Head Association (IPL) isn't simply a cricketing party; a perplexing biological system of key partners assume urgent parts in molding the association's stories, achievement, and heritage. At the core of this environment are the establishment proprietors, mentors, and players — people whose choices, systems, and exhibitions add to the association's remaining as one of the most observed T20 competitions universally. Grasping the elements, difficulties, and goals of these key partners gives a thorough perspective on the IPL's diverse nature.

Establishment proprietors, the visionary draftsmen of IPL groups, hold the reins of the association's fate. These people or consortiums, frequently addressing assorted ventures and foundations, put away cash as well as energy and key insight into their individual establishments. The responsibility for IPL group isn't just an undertaking; it is a social venture, an association with a city or district, and a promise to building a cricketing inheritance.

The establishment proprietors become the essence of their groups, typifying the expectations and desires of millions of fans. From Bollywood superstars like Shah Rukh Khan and Preity Zinta to business magnates, for example, Mukesh Ambani and Nita Ambani, the proprietors bring star power, impact, and business insight to the IPL. Their association reaches out past the meeting room; they are seen energetically applauding their groups from the stands, drawing in with fans via virtual entertainment, and turning into the public persona of their establishments.

Monetarily, claiming an IPL group is a high-stakes adventure. The establishment proprietors are liable for player pay rates, functional costs, and guaranteeing the generally monetary strength of their groups. The speculations stretch out past player acquisitions; they incorporate showcasing, brand fabricating, and making a fan-accommodating environment both in the arenas and in the computerized domain. The monetary progress of the IPL is intently attached to the capacity of establishment proprietors to adjust the books while handling cutthroat groups that catch the public's creative mind.

The bartering room turns into the milestone where establishment proprietors feature their essential ability. The choices made during the player barters shape the creation and strength of their crews. The monetary limitations, as directed by the compensation cap, force proprietors to go with determined decisions, gauging the worth of marquee players against the requirement for crew profundity. The effective establishment proprietors are the ones who find some kind of harmony between star power and group collaboration.

Past the monetary and key viewpoints, establishment proprietors add to the association's prosperity by cultivating a feeling of local area and having a place. The IPL has turned into a social peculiarity, and the possession bunches assume a significant part in supporting the close to home association fans have with their groups. The contribution of proprietors in local area drives, outreach programs, and charitable undertakings adds a human touch to the charming and impressive universe of the IPL.

Mentors, the strategic maestros uninvolved, shoulder the obligation of deciphering the vision of proprietors into on-field achievement. The job of a mentor in the IPL reaches out past customary training; it includes man-the executives, key preparation, and making a group culture that flourishes under tension. The instructing staff, frequently containing a blend of experienced cricketing minds and arising gifts, turns into the foundation of an effective IPL crusade.

The mentor's impact isn't restricted to the specialized parts of the game; it reaches out to player improvement, mental molding, and encouraging a triumphant mindset. The extraordinary timetable of the IPL, with its consecutive matches and high-pressure circumstances, requests a novel arrangement of abilities from the training staff. The capacity to peruse the game, pursue vital choices on the fly, and keep players spurred even with difficulties turns into a sign of fruitful mentors in the IPL.

The job of a mentor turns out to be considerably more basic in a configuration like T20, where fast reasoning and versatility are principal. The essential breaks during coordinates furnish mentors with an open door to recalibrate plans, survey resistance techniques, and pass basic messages on to players. The strategic discernment of a mentor frequently turns into the separating factor in firmly challenged matches, where a very much planned choice can influence the energy for a group.

Mentors likewise assume a significant part in ability recognizable proof and player improvement. The IPL has been a favorable place for arising gifts, giving a stage to youthful cricketers to grandstand their abilities on a worldwide stage. The examples of overcoming adversity of players like Hardik Pandya, Jasprit Bumrah, and Shubman Gill, who rose through the positions under the direction of their IPL mentors, feature the formative part of training in the association.

The connection between establishment proprietors and mentors is a sensitive dance of shared dreams and common trust. Proprietors depend mentors with the obligation of building serious groups, and mentors depend on the help and assets given by proprietors to execute their arrangements. The cooperative energy among proprietorship and training staff turns into a critical determinant of a group's prosperity, as found in the union showed by champion establishments throughout the long term.

Players, a definitive heroes on the field, are the main thrust behind the IPL's charm and fame. The association draws in a world of global and homegrown stars, changing each match into an exhibit of cricketing splendor. For players, the IPL isn't simply a competition; it is a phase where notorieties are made, heritages are cut, and dreams are understood.

The closeout room turns into a nerve-wracking field for players as they anticipate their destiny. The offering wars and the last sticker price connected to their names become markers of their apparent worth in the T20 market. From laid out worldwide stalwarts to youthful and arising abilities, players from assorted foundations meet in the bartering room, each holding onto desires of wearing the shades of an IPL establishment.

The monetary bonus related with the IPL is a huge inspiration for players. The association's financial ability, appeared in rewarding player agreements and under-writing open doors, draws in top ability from around the world. The IPL has turned into a sought-after objective for players, giving them monetary prizes as well as openness on a worldwide stage.

The presentation in the IPL frequently turns into a gauge of a player's T20 qualifications. Outcome in the association opens ways to other T20 associations universally, upgrading a player's attractiveness and making ready for global acknowledgment. On the other hand, disappointing exhibitions or wounds during the IPL can have repercussions on a player's general vocation direction.

The association's effect on the vocations of Indian players is especially signifi-cant. Youthful cricketers, addressing different states and locales, utilize the IPL as a venturing stone to worldwide cricket. The openness to high-pressure circum-stances, the chance to share the changing area with global stars, and the direction of experienced mentors add to the fast advancement of Indian gifts.

The abroad players, frequently filling in as marquee attractions, carry a world-wide flavor to the IPL. The presence of global cricketing symbols hoists the associ-ation's seriousness as well as improves its allure as a mixture of cricketing societies.

The IPL has turned into a stage where players from various nations structure obligations of kinship, rising above public competitions for the more prominent reason for T20 diversion.

The IPL's booking, with matches played in the nights and under floodlights, adds to the exhibition for players and fans the same. The electric environments in notable arenas like the Wankhede in Mumbai, the Eden Nurseries in Kolkata, and the M. Chinnaswamy Arena in Bangalore establish a climate that players relish. The thunder of the group, the music, and the dynamic environment add to the exceptional experience of playing in the IPL.

For establishment proprietors, mentors, and players the same, the IPL is a tireless trial of abilities, flexibility, and strength. The serious contest, combined with the capriciousness of T20 cricket, makes each season a rollercoaster ride. Achievement is estimated as far as game dominates as well as in the capacity to explore the difficulties of wounds, structure droops, and the strain cooker climate of knockout matches.

The association's effect reaches out past the cricketing field, affecting the existences of players and their families. The monetary security given by IPL contracts, combined with the openness and supports, changes the existences of numerous cricketers. The association has turned into an encouraging sign for trying cricketers, a stage where ability meets an open door, and dreams track down wings.

Chapter 2

Building the Blueprint

Building the outline of the Indian Head Association (IPL) is an excursion that interweaves development, scene, and cricketing ability. From its origin in 2008, the IPL has developed into a worldwide cricketing peculiarity, rethinking the scene of T20 cricket and setting new benchmarks in sports diversion. This plan, made by visionary managers, energetic establishment proprietors, and cricketing stalwarts, has changed how cricket is played as well as made a donning scene that resounds with crowds around the world.

At the core of the IPL's outline is the T20 design itself — a progressive idea that gathers the substance of cricket into a super charged, three-hour spectacle. The T20 design, described by its hazardous batting, key field positions, and creative bowling varieties, adjusts impeccably with the high speed, present day way of life. The IPL, subsequently, was considered as a vehicle to promote this configuration, bringing the fervor of T20 cricket to the very front of the brandishing scene.

The competition's construction, including establishments addressing various urban areas and districts, veers off from the conventional cricketing model. This deviation, in any case, is a masterstroke that upgrades the IPL's allure.

The city-based establishments not just carry a neighborhood flavor to the association yet additionally manufacture profound associations with fans who rally behind their host groups. The feeling of local pride, joined with the imbuement of worldwide cricketing stars, makes an extraordinary mix that spellbinds a different and worldwide crowd.

The diagram of the IPL consolidates a reasonable and cutthroat association design, where each group faces each and every other group two times in the co-operative stage. This design guarantees a fair and thorough assessment of groups, making way for serious contentions and critical conflicts. The association stage fills in as the pot where groups jar for positions, and the race for the season finisher compartments strengthens as the season advances.

The end of the season games, acquainted with add a knockout aspect to the competition, are an essential component of the IPL's diagram. The top groups from the association stage advance to the end of the season games, where each match turns into a virtual last. The Eliminator and Qualifier matches come full circle in the Fabulous Last, a definitive standoff to decide the IPL champions. The season finisher framework infuses an additional layer of show, guaranteeing that the fervor works to a crescendo as the competition arrives at its peak.

The idea of player barters, a noteworthy development, is a focal mainstay of the IPL's plan. The barterings, described by shut and open offering, infuse a component of flightiness and exhibition into the group building process. Establishments, equipped with foreordained financial plans, participate in offering battles to procure players, making a unique commercial center where cricketing gifts are esteemed and fortunes are made. The sale design has turned into an essential piece of the association's personality, transforming the group incorporating process into a scene that dazzles crowds and keeps fans as eager and anxious as ever.

The presentation of marquee players in the sales, frequently worldwide cricketing symbols, adds star power and worldwide enticement for the IPL. These marquee players, pursued for their cricketing ability and attractiveness, become the central purposes of offering wars. The closeouts, in this manner, are tied in with collecting a group as well as about making a story that reverberates with fans and partners the same. The marquee players bring cricketing greatness as well as a feeling of style and moxy, lifting the association's status to a worldwide brandishing spectacle.

The maintenance strategy, coordinated into the outline in later versions, gives establishments dependability and congruity. The capacity to hold a specific number of players from the past season permits groups to protect the center of their crews, sustaining a feeling of personality and reliability. The maintenance strategy likewise presents key intricacies, as establishments should choose which players to hold and which to deliver into the bartering pool. This component of dynamic adds a layer of interest to the group building process, guaranteeing that the elements of the association stay liquid and eccentric.

The Option to Match (RTM) card, presented in 2018, further improves the essential complexities of the sales. This card permits establishments to hold a player by matching the most noteworthy bid they get for that player in the closeout. The RTM card turns into a strategic instrument, and its use requires cautious thought. Establishments should gauge the benefit of holding a player against the chance to get new ability in the closeout. The RTM card infuses a component of tension, as groups decisively play their cards to keep up with crew congruity while likewise adjusting to the advancing elements of the association.

The essential breaks, one more development acquired from T20 cricket, are integrated into the outline to improve the watcher experience. These breaks furnish groups with a chance to reevaluate methodologies, make strategic changes, and participate in brief clusters. The essential breaks, frequently joined by diversion sections, add a unique component to the review insight, transforming each match into a spellbinding exhibition.

The global kind of the IPL, with players from various cricketing societies meeting, adds a cosmopolitan appeal to the association. The presence of abroad players hoists the opposition as well as transforms the IPL into a worldwide cricketing fair. The association turns into a mixture of ability, where players from various nations structure partnerships, share encounters, and add to the cross-fertilization of cricketing styles. The different mix of societies enhances the association's story, making it a festival of cricket on a worldwide stage.

The IPL's outline isn't restricted to the cricketing field; it stretches out to the energetic airs made in notable arenas. The choice of scenes, with their verifiable importance and ability to have enormous groups, is an essential part of the association's outline. From the humming Wankhede Arena in Mumbai to the electric Eden Nurseries in Kolkata, every setting turns into a theater where the show of T20 cricket unfurls. The air, filled by enthusiastic fans, music, and diversion, adds to the general scene and changes each match into a fair.

The association's diagram consolidates a hearty computerized methodology, utilizing innovation to expand crowd commitment. The IPL's true site, versatile applications, and web-based entertainment stages become virtual fields where fans associate with the association. The incorporation of live streaming, ongoing updates, and intelligent highlights guarantees that the IPL stays open to a worldwide crowd. The association's computerized presence intensifies its range as well as makes an all year commitment with fans, supporting interest past the competition window.

Lately, the IPL's obligation to supportability and social obligation has turned into a vital piece of its outline. Drives like "Green Games" plan to limit the biological impression of the association, with measures, for example, eco-accommodating arenas, squander the board projects, and mindfulness crusades. The IPL's job as a capable donning element is reflected in its endeavors to contribute emphatically to the climate and society.

The IPL's diagram, based on the groundwork of development and diversion, has changed the cricketing scene as well as raised the association to the situation with a social peculiarity. The combination of cricketing greatness, star power, and worldwide allure has transformed the IPL into a donning party that rises above topographical and social limits. The outline, ceaselessly developing and adjusting to the requests of the cutting edge crowd, guarantees that the IPL stays a benchmark in the realm of sports diversion.

The association's outline reaches out past the limits of the battleground; it includes the fantasies about yearning cricketers, the feelings of intense fans, and the desires of establishment proprietors. It is a material where cricketing masterfulness meets vital brightness, making a magnum opus that unfurls each season with reestablished power. The IPL's outline is a demonstration of the visionaries who considered the association, the partners who contributed enthusiasm and assets, and the players who rejuvenated the plan on the consecrated turf. As the IPL keeps on enchanting crowds and reclassify the forms of present day cricket, the diagram remains as a reference point of development, motivation, and the tenacious quest for brandishing greatness.

2.1 Pre-auction preparations by franchises

The pre-closeout ease in the Indian Head Association (IPL) is a period of fastidious preparation, key consultations, and determined choices for establishments. It is a basic crossroads where group the board, proprietors, and training staff team up to characterize the crew's outline for the impending season. The pre-closeout arrangements are not only about player acquisitions; they envelop a thorough system that includes player maintenance, discharge, vital preparation, and monetary contemplations, all pointed toward building a reasonable and cutthroat group that can explore the difficulties of T20 cricket.

Player maintenance fills in as the central stage in an establishment's pre-closeout arrangements. The choice to hold players includes a fragile harmony between faithfulness to existing crew individuals and the quest for new ability. Establishments should cautiously assess the presentation, structure, and generally speaking worth of each held player, taking into account their abilities to cricket as well as their attractiveness and fan bid. The maintenance interaction establishes the vibe for a group's progression and personality, giving a brief look into the center that the establishment means to safeguard.

Vital decision-production during the pre-sell off stage additionally incorporates the arrival of players who might not have satisfied hopes or whose administrations are considered excess to the group's necessities. The arrival of players opens up monetary space and permits establishments to go into the bartering room with monetary adaptability. The choice to deliver players requires a mix of cricketing keenness and monetary reasonability, as establishments should work out some kind of harmony between enhancing their crew and dealing with the limitations of the compensation cap.

The compensation cap, a focal component in the pre-sell off arrangements, forces monetary limitations on establishments, adding a component of procedure and asset the board to the group building process. Each establishment is designated a foreordained financial plan that they should stick to during the bartering. The compensation cap forestalls the rise of cricketing governments and guarantees a level battleground, as groups should pursue sensible choices inside the monetary limits set by the association.

The portion of the compensation cap turns into an essential activity where establishments should choose how to disperse their monetary assets across various player classifications. Marquee players, arising gifts, and utility players each accompany their own sticker prices, and the pre-sell off arrangements include a fastidious examination of player valuations. Establishments frequently utilize a mix of information investigation, exploring reports, and cricketing bits of knowledge to evaluate a player's reasonable worth and decide the ideal financial plan portion.

The pre-closeout arrangements stretch out to the production of a list of things to get — an essential report that frames the particular player necessities for each group. This list of things to get is an impression of the group's requirements, taking into account factors like group creation, playing conditions, and the systems utilized by rival establishments. The list of things to get turns into a directing report for group the executives during the closeout, assisting them with focusing on targets and pursue educated choices in the intensity regarding offering wars.

In the mission for player acquisitions, establishments additionally participate in exchange conversations and discussions during the pre-sell off stage. Player exchanges permit groups to address explicit holes in their crews by trading players with different establishments. The exchange elements add an additional layer of intricacy to the pre-sell off arrangements, as groups should explore talks, evaluate the worth of players in the exchange market, and work out agreements that line up with their essential targets.

The job of information examination in pre-closeout arrangements couldn't possibly be more significant. Establishments utilize analysts, examiners, and cricket specialists to do the math, dissect player exhibitions, and distinguish likely deals in the closeout pool. The utilization of information driven bits of knowledge permits groups to pursue informed choices, survey player commitments past customary measurements, and reveal unexpected, yet invaluable treasures who might not have snatched features however have the traits required for T20 achievement.

The pre-sell off stage likewise includes a cautious investigation of the qualities and shortcomings of opponent establishments. Groups concentrate on the crew sytheses, systems, and possible focuses of different establishments, expecting to acquire an upper hand in the closeout room. The closeout, portrayed by shut and open offering, expects establishments to remain dexterous and adjust their systems in light of the elements of the room. Information on rival groups' systems turns into an important resource in making fast, essential choices.

The Option to Match (RTM) cards, a development presented in the IPL barters, add one more layer of intricacy to the pre-closeout arrangements. The choice on when and how to involve the RTM cards turns into an essential thought for establishments. Groups should assess the market worth of their held players, expect to contend offers in the bartering, and decisively convey the RTM cards to hold key donors from the past season. The use of RTM cards requires premonition and strategic discernment, as groups try to work out some kind of harmony between crew progression and new acquisitions.

The pre-sell off stage isn't just about on-field procedures yet in addition about brand building and showcasing. Establishments participate in special exercises, divulge group shirts, and construct publicity around their crews to create fan fervor. The promoting efforts are intended to make a buzz, produce ticket deals, and improve the general brand worth of the establishment. The pre-closeout stage, thusly, turns into a comprehensive activity that includes both the cricketing and business aspects of the IPL.

The sale elements, represented by the principles laid out in the pre-sell off stage, unfurl as a high-stakes theater where establishments bid for players in a serious free for all. The shut offering, where groups submit fixed envelopes for explicit players, adds a component of mystery and shock to the procedures. The open offering that follows is portrayed by extraordinary ever changing offering battles, with groups competing to get their ideal players at the most ideal costs.

The pre-sell off arrangements come full circle in the closeout room, where group proprietors, mentors, and examiners team up to execute their techniques. The barker arranges the procedures, establishing a climate that is both extraordinary and dynamic. The essential breaks during the sale furnish establishments with brief breaks to reevaluate their arrangements, talk with group the board, and recalibrate their offering procedures.

The outcome of pre-closeout arrangements is at last estimated by the creation of the last crew. The bartering results mirror the viability of an establishment's methodology, the incentive for cash got in player acquisitions, and the general seriousness of the crew. The last crew turns into the material whereupon the group will paint its excursion in the impending time of the IPL.

The pre-closeout stage, with its complex preparation and key contemplations, establishes the vibe for the whole IPL season. The choices made during this period affect group elements, fan commitment, and the general progress of the establishment. It is a stage where the cricketing discernment of group the board merges with monetary reasonability, vital premonition, and a profound comprehension of the steadily developing T20 scene.

2.2 Budget considerations and team strategies

Spending plan contemplations and group techniques structure the essence of an establishment's methodology in the Indian Head Association (IPL), where the elements of player barters request a sensitive harmony between monetary reasonability and cricketing desire. The distributed compensation cap, a monetary limitation that shapes the association's serious scene, turns into a vital element impacting group techniques. Establishments go into the bartering room equipped with foreordained spending plans, and how they explore this monetary landscape, settle on essential choices, and fabricate a serious crew decides their progress in the T20 spectacle.

The compensation cap, a foundation of the IPL's monetary design, puts a roof on the sum an establishment can spend on player pay rates during the bartering. The cap guarantees equality among groups, forestalling a situation where monetary muscle alone decides achievement. Each establishment is doled out a particular spending plan, and inside this monetary system, they should collect a crew that finds some kind of harmony between star power, arising gifts, and utility players.

Spending plan contemplations force establishments to go with key choices on player maintenance, delivery, and enlistment. The distribution of the compensation cap turns into a chess game where establishments should evaluate the worth of every player, gauge their commitments, and pursue choices that line up with the group's essential goals. The sensitive difficult exercise includes deciding the monetary worth of marquee players, holding center crew individuals, and procuring new ability acceptable for the spending plan imperatives.

Techniques in regards to player maintenance are impacted by a mix of on-field execution, brand worth, and fan bid. Marquee players, frequently global cricketing symbols, convey more exorbitant cost labels because of their double commitment — both on the field and off it, concerning attractiveness and fan commitment. Establishments should survey whether holding such players lines up with their financial plan and group building methodology, taking into account the harmony between cricketing effect and business esteem.

Financial plan contemplations likewise assume a part in the choice to deliver players. The arrival of players opens up monetary space, giving establishments monetary adaptability during the closeout. Be that as it may, this choice requires a nuanced approach, as groups should gauge the exhibition and capability of delivered players against the open door cost of entering the sale with a bigger tote. The delivery system turns into a sensitive harmony between cost-cutting and crew enhancement.

The mission for a fair crew inside the compensation cap imperatives drives group techniques during the bartering. Establishments enter the offering battle with clear goals — recognizing key jobs, focusing on unambiguous player classifications, and sticking to monetary impediments. The group's masterful course of action includes focusing on areas of need, evaluating player valuations, and staying versatile to the unique idea of the closeout room.

The job of information examination becomes essential in financial plan contemplations and group methodologies. Establishments utilize analysts, investigators, and cricket specialists to evaluate player exhibitions, recognize likely deals, and advance spending plan allotment. Information driven bits of knowledge give a logical establishment to navigation, assisting groups with distinguishing players whose measurable commitments may not be promptly clear yet line up with the group's essential objectives.

Methodologies additionally spin around unfamiliar and uncapped players, each presenting remarkable difficulties and open doors. Abroad players, frequently marquee names, accompany greater cost labels and effect the unfamiliar player share, adding a layer of intricacy to spending plan contemplations. Establishments should choose how to convey their abroad player openings decisively, offsetting star power with crew profundity and sticking to financial plan requirements.

The incorporation of uncapped players, then again, presents a component of unconventionality. Establishments frequently strive for arising gifts, perceiving the potential for uncovering unlikely treasures who can convey esteem past their sticker prices. The offering battles for uncapped players become a mix of instinct, risk-taking, and vital computation, as groups survey the unquantifiable potential and long haul effect of these youthful cricketers.

Financial plan contemplations stretch out past player pay rates to envelop group the board, instructing staff, and other functional costs. Establishments should distribute assets prudently, guaranteeing that they have the fundamental care staff, offices, and framework to expand the exhibition of their crew. The monetary discipline stretches out to regions like travel, convenience, and special exercises, adding to the by and large monetary strength of the establishment.

The Option to Match (RTM) card, presented in 2014, further confuses spending plan contemplations and group systems. This card permits establishments to hold a specific number of players from their past season's crew by matching the most noteworthy bid they get for those players in the sale. The essential utilization of RTM cards includes assessing the market worth of held players, expecting cutthroat offers, and decisively conveying the cards to keep up with crew congruity without surpassing monetary cutoff points.

Group techniques additionally include the planning of offers and vital breaks during the sale. Establishments should measure the elements of the sale room, evaluate the opposition for explicit players, and decisively bid to get their objectives inside financial plan requirements. The essential breaks furnish groups with brief breaks to reevaluate plans, talk with group the board, and recalibrate offering systems, guaranteeing that financial plan contemplations stay lined up with the general group building methodology.

Establishments frequently embrace various methodologies in light of their particular monetary positions and long haul objectives. A few groups might zero in on securing laid out stars to fabricate a cutthroat crew, while others might focus on youth and potential, planning to develop a group for supported achievement. The mix of experienced players and arising gifts turns into an essential decision that mirrors an establishment's vision, assets, and obligation to long haul achievement.

Spending plan contemplations and group procedures likewise reach out to mid-season moves and player exchanges. Establishments survey their crew's presentation and distinguish areas of progress during the competition. The mid-season move window permits groups to address these holes by getting players from different establishments. The choice to exchange players, as different parts of group methodology, includes a cautious assessment of crew elements, spending plan requirements, and the quest for key objectives.

2.3 Role of team think tanks in strategizing for the auction

The job of group think tanks in planning for the Indian Chief Association (IPL) closeout is a dynamic and complex perspective that assumes a vital part in molding the fortunes of establishments. The research organization, containing group proprietors, mentors, examiners, and specialists, teams up to make an exhaustive diagram that lines up with the group's vision, assets, and long haul goals. This aggregate knowledge turns into the directing power behind an establishment's decision-production during the bartering, including player assessments, financial plan contemplations, and vital preparation.

One of the essential obligations of the group think tank is player exploring and assessment. The research organization utilizes a blend of information examination, cricketing skill, and exploring organizations to evaluate the presentation, structure, and capability of players accessible in the closeout pool. The information driven approach includes doing the math, investigating insights, and recognizing designs that may not be quickly obvious, giving a logical premise to player evaluations.

The research organization's job in player assessments stretches out past conventional measurements to incorporate subjective factors like disposition, flexibility, and wellness. Cricketing specialists inside the research organization contribute experiences in light of how they might interpret the game and the particular necessities of T20 cricket.

The incorporation of both quantitative and subjective appraisals permits establishments to settle on all around informed choices that go past crude insights.

Planning for the bartering includes ordering players in light of their jobs — marquee players, all-rounders, expert batsmen, bowlers, and arising abilities. The research organization decides the group's needs and areas of need, delineating a system that guarantees a reasonable and serious crew. The essential arrangement of player classifications with group necessities turns into a basic part of the research organization's job in forming the bartering technique.

Spending plan contemplations structure a critical piece of the research organization's job, with monetary specialists and examiners teaming up to enhance the portion of the compensation cap. The research organization should work out some kind of harmony between getting marquee players, tending to explicit crew needs, and sticking to monetary limitations. The monetary discipline guarantees that the group can fabricate a cutthroat crew inside the distributed financial plan, forestalling overspending that could influence the group's drawn out manageability.

The research organization's essential arranging includes choices on player maintenance and delivery. The research organization surveys the benefit of holding players from the past season, taking into account factors like on-field commitments, attractiveness, and fan request. All the while, choices on player discharges require an insightful methodology, as the research organization considers the exhibition and capability of every player in contrast to the background of spending plan limitations and vital objectives.

The Option to Match (RTM) cards, an essential device presented in the bartering elements, add one more layer of intricacy to the research organization's job. The research organization should settle on choices on when and how to send the RTM cards, taking into account the market worth of held players, the opposition in the sale room, and the general crew building system. The use of RTM cards turns into a strategic move that requires prescience and a comprehension of the serious scene.

The research organization's essential arranging likewise stretches out to group structure, taking into account the mix of experienced players and arising abilities. The research organization should settle on the ideal blend that lines up with the group's vision and long haul targets. The determination of abroad players, a basic perspective in a restricted unfamiliar player portion, turns into an essential choice that includes recognizing the right harmony between star power and crew profundity.

The research organization's job during the bartering itself is dynamic and calls for continuous independent direction. The shut offering stage, where groups submit fixed envelopes for explicit players, requests vital premonition as establishments make introductory offers in light of their foreordained player valuations.

The research organization should be deft and versatile, answering the developing elements of the sale room and changing techniques in light of contending offers and economic situations.

Vital breaks during the closeout give the research organization brief breaks to rethink plans, talk with group the board, and recalibrate offering techniques. These breaks become critical in a climate portrayed by serious offering wars and quick direction. The research organization use these essential breaks to guarantee that the group stays on track with its general sale technique and doesn't go amiss from the foreordained arrangement.

The research organization's job isn't restricted to player acquisitions during the sale; it reaches out to mid-season moves and player exchanges. The research organization evaluates the group's exhibition, recognizes areas of progress, and participates in talks to address explicit holes in the crew. The essential changes made through mid-season moves and exchanges mirror the research organization's capacity to adjust to the developing necessities of the group and benefit from valuable open doors in the player market.

Information investigation stays a foundation of the research organization's job, giving a hearty groundwork to independent direction. Factual models, execution measurements, and prescient examination add to player assessments, vital preparation, and financial plan enhancement. The mix of innovation permits the research organization to remain in front of patterns, distinguish arising gifts, and reveal expected deals in the player market.

Past the closeout room, the research organization's job stretches out to group the executives during the IPL season. The research organization works together with the training staff to guarantee that the group's technique is lined up with on-field strategies. The research organization's choices during the bartering impact the general group culture, playing style, and the account the establishment wishes to convey. The research organization's impact saturates each part of the group's excursion, from crew working to on-handle execution.

The research organization likewise assumes a pivotal part in brand building, showcasing, and fan commitment. The choices made during the sale, like player acquisitions and vital decisions, add to the general account and personality of the establishment. The research organization works together with the showcasing group to make limited time crusades, uncover group shirts, and draw in with fans, fabricating a brand that resounds past the cricketing field.

Chapter 3

Marquee Players and Mega Bids

Marquee players and super offers are indispensable parts of the scene that is the Indian Chief Association (IPL) sell off. These components add a layer of style, star power, and expectation to the offering system, transforming the bartering room into a theater where cricketing symbols order consideration and establishments strive furiously to get their administrations. The idea of marquee players and uber offers adds to the bigger story of the IPL, mixing cricketing ability with attractiveness, and forming the association into a worldwide donning party.

Marquee players, frequently global cricketing symbols or achieved Indian stars, possess an extraordinary spot in the IPL closeout elements. These players are not only pursued for their on-field commitments yet in addition for their capacity to draw in fans, backers, and media consideration. The marquee players bring a degree of star power that rises above cricketing limits, lifting the association's status and appeal to a worldwide crowd.

The expectation encompassing marquee players starts a long time before the sale, as establishments and fans enthusiastically anticipate the revealing of the player list.

The incorporation of cricketing legends or high-profile players produces buzz, hypothesis, and conversations about potential offering wars. The marquee players become the central marks of pre-closeout examinations, with intellectuals and specialists foreseeing the effect they could have on the fortunes of establishments.

Super offers, described by high financial qualities and serious offering wars, are a characteristic outcome of the presence of marquee players in the sale pool. Establishments enter the closeout with foreordained spending plans, yet the charm of getting a marquee player frequently prompts forceful offering that outperforms starting valuations. Uber offers make a climate of fervor and strain in the sale room, as group proprietors, mentors, and planners take part in essential fights to get the mark of a sought after player.

The uber offers mirror the monetary capability of establishments as well as the essential significance put on specific players. Groups perceive the double effect that marquee players bring — upgraded on-field execution and elevated off-field perceivability. The super offers, in this manner, become vital interests in both cricketing achievement and brand building. The sticker price connected to a marquee player reflects their cricketing worth as well as their attractiveness and capacity to draw swarms.

The sale elements for marquee players frequently include a mix of shut and open offering. The shut offering stage, where groups submit fixed envelopes for explicit players, adds a component of mystery and shock to the procedures. The fixed offers are uncovered at the same time, elevating the show as the most noteworthy bidder is disclosed. The open offering that follows is portrayed by extraordinary volatile offering battles, with establishments competing to outbid one another and secure the administrations of marquee players.

The super offers are not restricted to global stars; Indian players who have left an imprint in worldwide cricket or those with a huge fan following frequently order significant aggregates. The wild contest for marquee Indian players reflects the cricket-insane country's enthusiasm for the game and the profound association that fans have with their local legends. Super offers for Indian players become a showing of an establishment's obligation to building a group that resounds with the neighborhood crowd.

The idea of marquee players and uber offers likewise converges with the maintenance strategy presented in the IPL. Establishments have the choice to hold a specific number of players from their past season's crew, and marquee players frequently highlight conspicuously in these maintenance choices. The maintenance of a marquee player guarantees steadiness in the crew as well as turns into an essential move to hold a player who encapsulates the establishment's personality and reverberates with the fan base.

The super offers add to the monetary biological system of the IPL, making a commercial center where players are esteemed for their cricketing abilities as well as for their more extensive effect on the association's business achievement. The monetary elements of super offers have a flowing impact, affecting player valuations no matter how you look at it. The progress of super offers likewise prompts establishments to reevaluate their procedures, prompting a recalibration of financial plans and sale strategies.

The uber offers for marquee players frequently include establishments going past their usual ranges of familiarity, extending their spending plans to get the administrations of a cricketing genius. The essential analytics incorporates evaluating the drawn out effect of such super offers in the group's seriousness, image worth, and fan commitment. The choice to make a super offered isn't simply a monetary exchange; it is an assertion of purpose, an exhibition of an establishment's desire to overwhelm on and off the field.

The achievement or disappointment of uber offers turns into a storyline inside the bigger account of the IPL. On the off chance that a marquee player satisfies the hopes set by the uber bid, it turns into an approval of the establishment's essential insight and a lift to the group's exhibition and attractiveness. On the other hand, in the event that a marquee player neglects to convey, it brings up issues about the insight of the super offered and its effect in the group's general structure.

The effect of marquee players and super offers stretches out past the battleground to the association's general account. The presence of cricketing legends or high-profile players turns into a showcasing resource, impacting TV viewership, ticket deals, and sponsorship bargains. The uber offers produce titles, flash discussions, and add to the buzz encompassing the IPL, making a feeling of expectation and fervor paving the way to the competition.

The examples of overcoming adversity of marquee players in the IPL further lift their status in the cricketing scene. Exhibitions in the association, combined with the perceivability and stage given by the IPL, upgrade the worldwide acknowledgment of marquee players. The IPL turns into a phase where cricketing symbols feature their abilities, engage fans, and make a permanent imprint on the association's set of experiences.

3.1 Analysis of marquee players in the auction

The examination of marquee players in the Indian Chief Association (IPL) close-out is a nuanced and key undertaking that includes assessing the effect, worth, and likely commitments of high-profile players to the outcome of establishments. Marquee players, frequently global cricketing symbols or achieved Indian stars, convey an extraordinary charm that rises above their on-field capacities. The examination envelops different features, including cricketing ability, attractiveness, fan bid, and the likely impact of these players in a group's exhibition, image, and by and large story in the association.

One urgent part of the examination is surveying the on-field execution and cricketing qualifications of marquee players. Establishments dig into the factual chronicles, looking at a player's record in T20 cricket, late structure, flexibility to various circumstances, and capacity to perform under tension. Information examination assume a critical part in this stage, giving bits of knowledge into a player's batting, bowling, and handling exhibitions, as well as their effect in unambiguous match circumstances.

The verifiable exhibition of marquee players in past releases of the IPL turns into a basic benchmark for examination. A history of steady exhibitions, match-dominating commitments, and the capacity to adjust to the remarkable requests of T20 cricket are factors that upgrade a player's worth. Establishments look for players who can convey individual splendor as well as add to the general outcome of the group.

Attractiveness and off-field influence structure one more component of the examination. Marquee players bring a degree of star power that reaches out past the cricketing field, making them important resources as far as sponsorship bargains, special exercises, and expanding the establishment's worldwide allure. The attractiveness examination includes assessing a player's image esteem, web-based entertainment presence, and the possibility to draw in supports, subsequently adding to the monetary wellbeing and business progress of the establishment.

The fan allure of marquee players is a vital thought. Players with a huge fan following, both locally and universally, carry an exceptional energy to the group. The presence of cricketing symbols in the crew draws in viewership as well as cultivates a more profound close to home association with fans. The investigation includes understanding the segment reach of a player's fan base and the possible effect on ticket deals, product, and in general fan commitment.

The essential attack of marquee players inside a group's organization is a basic part of the investigation. Establishments should evaluate whether a marquee player lines up with the group's playing style, supplements the current crew, and fills explicit jobs or holes. The collaboration between a marquee player and the general group technique becomes instrumental in deciding the outcome of the obtaining.

Financial plan contemplations assume a huge part in the examination of marquee players. While these players bring enormous worth, establishments should work out some kind of harmony between getting marquee names and dealing with the general financial plan for player compensations. The monetary interest in a marquee player ought to line up with the group's general system, guaranteeing that the financial plan is streamlined to fabricate a reasonable and cutthroat crew.

The sale elements add one more layer to the investigation of marquee players. The shut and open offering stages request key discernment and constant independent direction.

Establishments should be lithe in the sale room, adjusting their offering systems in light of the serious scene, other group's goals, and economic situations. The capacity to go with educated choices in the intensity regarding offering wars is a demonstration of the viability of the examination led by the establishment's research organization.

The Option to Match (RTM) cards, an essential device presented in the IPL closeout, further confounds the examination. Establishments should choose when and how to send the RTM cards for marquee players held from the past season. The choice includes assessing the market worth of held players, expecting to contend offers, and decisively utilizing the RTM cards to keep up with crew coherence without surpassing monetary cutoff points.

The examples of overcoming adversity of marquee players in past IPL seasons act as contextual analyses for examination. Establishments evaluate how these players have performed under various group conditions, the board styles, and playing conditions. Understanding the flexibility and strength of marquee players gives bits of knowledge into their likely commitments to another group.

The examination of marquee players additionally stretches out to the expected effect in group elements. The presence of a cricketing legend or high-profile player in the changing area can impact the resolve, certainty, and execution of the whole crew. Establishments should assess how a marquee player lines up with the group's way of life, initiative design, and the tutoring job they can play for arising gifts.

Wounds and wellness concerns are extra components that variable into the investigation of marquee players. Establishments should survey the injury history of these players, their momentum wellness levels, and the possible effect on their accessibility for the whole IPL season. The examination incorporates a gamble evaluation, guaranteeing that the interest in a marquee player isn't undermined by successive wounds or wellness issues.

The social and geological attack of marquee players inside the city or locale addressed by the establishment is a perspective frequently thought to be in the examination. Players who resound with the nearby culture and ethos can become notable figures, producing a more profound association with fans. The social arrangement adds an elusive component to the examination, adding to the general story and character of the establishment.

The examination of marquee players is a continuous cycle that reaches out past the closeout room. When a marquee player is obtained, establishments should consistently evaluate their presentation, effect, and flexibility all through the IPL season. Mid-season evaluations permit groups to make vital changes, address any difficulties, and streamline the use of marquee players chasing on-field achievement.

3.2 High-profile bidding wars and record-breaking deals

High-profile offering wars and record-breaking bargains are mark components of the Indian Head Association (IPL) sell off, changing the occasion into a high-stakes display that enraptures cricket fans and relaxed watchers the same. These offering wars, described by extreme rivalry among establishments competing for sought-after players, and the ensuing record-breaking bargains, shape the association's account as well as highlight the monetary elements, vital keenness, and the advancing scene of T20 cricket.

The offering wars unfurl as establishments go into the closeout room equipped with brilliant courses of action, player lists of things to get, and apportioned spending plans. The air is accused of expectation as the barker presents marquee players, making way for serious offering fights. Establishments take part in an essential dance, evaluating the opposition, measuring player valuations, and settling on fast choices that can have extensive ramifications for the impending IPL season.

The shut offering stage denotes the beginning of the great profile offering wars. Establishments submit fixed envelopes containing their offers for explicit players, adding a component of mystery and technique to the procedures. The fixed offers are disclosed all the while, uncovering the most noteworthy bidder for every player. The shut offering establishes the underlying vibe for the closeout, with establishments taking key actions to get vital participants while sticking to their foreordained financial plans.

As the sale changes to the open offering stage, the force arrives at its pinnacle. Establishments participate in open, ongoing offering battles, with each bid setting off counter-offers as groups contend to get the administrations of desired players. The open offering stage is portrayed by quick fire choices, key moves, and an obvious need to get going as establishments mean to outbid their opponents and collect a serious crew.

The high-profile offering wars frequently rotate around marquee players — cricketing symbols, match-victors, and players with a worldwide fan following. The star force of these players adds a layer of charm to the bartering, standing out from fans, supporters, and media. Establishments perceive the double effect of marquee players — on-field commitments and off-field attractiveness — and participate in wild offering battles to get the marks of these cricketing stars.

The offering battles for marquee players frequently lead to uber offers, breaking records and rethinking the monetary benchmarks of the IPL. Establishments, driven by the craving to get major advantages and pioneers, stretch their spending plans, bringing about eye-watering aggregates being spent on individual players.

The uber offers mirror the monetary muscle of establishments as well as highlight the top notch put on specific players considered irreplaceable to a group's prosperity.

The elements of high-profile offering wars reach out past marquee players to incorporate arising abilities and utility players who catch the creative mind of establishments. The cutthroat idea of the sale room guarantees that even moderately obscure players can turn into the focal point of extreme offering fights. Establishments survey potential, ability, and explicit ranges of abilities, participating in offering battles to uncover unlikely treasures who can make significant commitments to the group.

The Option to Match (RTM) cards, presented in the IPL closeout, add vital layers to the offering wars. Establishments, having held players from the past season, can utilize RTM cards to counter offers and hold explicit players by matching the most elevated bid in the bartering. The essential organization of RTM cards turns into a strategic thought for establishments, adding a component of unconventionality to the offering elements.

Record-breaking bargains in the IPL sell off frequently make features and become arguments that resound past the cricketing local area. The monetary benchmarks set by these arrangements mirror the advancing financial aspects of T20 cricket, the association's worldwide allure, and the eagerness of establishments to put resources into headliners. Record-breaking bargains raise the situation with players as well as add to the story of the IPL as a head cricketing association.

The record-breaking bargains are not restricted to marquee players; they likewise stretch out to uncapped players who draw in huge consideration because of their exhibitions in homegrown and T20 associations. The ability of establishments to put significant sums in arising gifts addresses the association's accentuation on youth, potential, and the conviction that specific uncapped players can become major advantages.

The procedures utilized by establishments in high-profile offering wars are diverse. Establishments should adjust the quest for headliners with the need to fabricate a decent and cutthroat crew. The essential list of things to get made during the pre-closeout stage turns into a directing report, assisting establishments with focusing on targets, survey player valuations, and settle on educated choices in the intensity regarding offering wars.

Information examination assumes a critical part in the essential decision-production during offering wars. Establishments utilize analysts, examiners, and cricket specialists to evaluate player exhibitions, recognize likely deals, and grasp the factual subtleties that go past customary measurements. The utilization of information driven experiences gives a logical establishment to direction, assisting groups with distinguishing players whose measurable commitments may not be promptly obvious.

The techniques in high-profile offering wars additionally include perusing the room, understanding the goals of opponent establishments, and adjusting to the powerful idea of the closeout. Establishments should be nimble, responsive, and ready to recalibrate their procedures in light of the unfurling offering elements. The capacity to make quick, essential choices is a sign of effective establishments in the cutthroat climate of the IPL sell off.

The progress of high-profile offering wars is estimated by the securing of head-liners as well as by the general intensity and equilibrium of the crew. Establishments should explore the monetary imperatives of the compensation cap, upgrade their spending plans, and guarantee that the super offers for marquee players don't think twice about profundity and equilibrium of the group. A definitive objective is to gather a crew that can battle for the IPL title.

The effect of high-profile offering wars is felt during the bartering as well as all through the IPL season. The players procured in these offering wars convey the heaviness of assumptions, and their exhibitions on the field become firmly examined. The achievement or disappointment of high-profile acquisitions adds to the account of the IPL, molding the impression of establishments, players, and the general intensity of the association.

3.3 Impact of marquee players on team composition and fanbase

The effect of marquee players in group organization and fanbase is a complex and vital part of the Indian Head Association (IPL), where the presence of cricketing symbols essentially impacts the essential elements of establishments and shapes the close to home association with fans. Marquee players, frequently worldwide stars or achieved Indian cricketers, bring a remarkable mix of on-field ability, attractive-ness, and star power that resounds all through the association.

One of the essential effects of marquee players in group structure is their capacity to act as the support around which the crew is constructed. Establishments decisively anchor their group creation by getting marquee players who succeed in their singular jobs as well as add to the general equilibrium and methodology of the group. The presence of a marquee player can shape the whole playing XI, impacting the determination of correlative players who line up with the headliner's assets and style of play.

Marquee players frequently accept positions of authority inside their separate groups, filling in as commanders or key leaders on the field. The initiative effect stretches out past strategic choices to include the group's way of life, resolve, and flexibility. Marquee players set the vibe for the crew, exemplifying the establishment's ethos and giving a wellspring of motivation to colleagues. The influential position of marquee players is an essential thought that impacts group creation and elements.

The impact of marquee players in group organization likewise stretches out to the batting and bowling orders. Establishments decisively position marquee players in the arrangement, taking into account their favored jobs, assets, and the match circumstance. The effect of a marquee player's presence in the top request can be groundbreaking, giving a strong groundwork or speedy beginnings that set the vibe for the innings. Likewise, marquee bowlers are frequently sent in a calculated way, with their overs urgent in forming the group's cautious or forceful systems.

Past on-field commitments, marquee players assume a urgent part in molding the off-field personality and attractiveness of an establishment. The fanbase influence is maybe most articulated in such manner. The securing of a cricketing symbol draws in existing fans as well as can possibly widen the group's allure, contacting new crowds and socioeconomics. Marquee players become the substance of the establishment, driving ticket deals, stock buys, and generally speaking fan commitment.

The effect of marquee players on the fanbase is obvious in the close to home association they fashion with allies. Fans frequently foster profound connections to marquee players, rooting for their victories and feeling for their difficulties. The presence of a darling cricketing symbol can make a feeling of dependability and enthusiasm among fans, cultivating a lively and committed fanbase that rises above topographical limits.

The attractiveness of marquee players altogether adds to the monetary outcome of establishments. Backers and sponsors are attracted to the star power and worldwide allure of these players, prompting worthwhile support arrangements, organizations, and marking potential open doors. The effect in the group's income streams is significant, with marquee players filling in as important resources in drawing in supports who try to adjust their image to the prevalence and mystique of cricketing symbols.

The effect in group organization and fanbase is especially articulated when marquee players are additionally famous skippers. The position of authority adds an additional layer of impact, as the chief turns into the substance of the establishment, driving from the front in both on-field exhibitions and key direction. The effect of a famous chief reaches out past cricketing abilities to incorporate characteristics like charm, motivation, and the capacity to excite the group and fanbase.

The essential obtaining of marquee players frequently includes cautious thought of their accessibility all through the IPL season. Global responsibilities, public group obligations, and different variables can influence a marquee player's cooperation in the association. Establishments should explore these contemplations while building their crews, guaranteeing that the marquee players they put resources into are accessible for a huge part of the time to give steady effect.

The effect of marquee players in group structure is additionally apparent yet to be determined between experienced stars and arising gifts. The presence of cricketing symbols gives a learning a valuable open door to youthful and arising players, who can profit from the mentorship, direction, and shared encounters of marquee players. The essential consideration of arising gifts close by marquee players guarantees the progression of progress and the development of an ability pipeline for what's to come.

Group elements are essentially affected by the degree of brotherhood and co-operative energy inside the crew. The effect of marquee players in group organization isn't simply restricted to their singular exhibitions yet stretches out to their capacity to cultivate a positive group climate. The brotherhood between marquee players and their partners adds to a durable unit that can endure the tensions of a requesting T20 competition.

The effect on the fanbase is likewise impacted by the openness and commitment of marquee players through web-based entertainment and different stages. Players who effectively associate with fans, share bits of knowledge into their lives, and take part in special exercises add to an energetic and involved fan local area. The effect of marquee players on the fanbase is improved when players become cricketing symbols as well as engaging characters who fans can interface with on an individual level.

The essential maintenance of marquee players starting with one season then onto the next is a demonstration of the drawn out influence they have in group piece and fanbase. Establishments put resources into holding these players for their cricketing abilities as well as for their persevering through impact in group culture, authority, and the profound association they have laid out with fans. The effect of marquee players goes past a solitary season, adding to the establishment's personality and heritage.

The effect of marquee players in group creation and fanbase additionally includes contemplations of group culture and ethos. Establishments decisively select players whose values line up with the ethos of the group, making a strong unit with a common obligation to progress. Marquee players who embrace the way of life of the establishment and effectively add to group building endeavors lastingly affect group elements.

The fanbase influence isn't exclusively subject to on-handle exhibitions; the direct of marquee players off the field additionally impacts public discernment. Players who participate in generous exercises, local area outreach, and other social drives add to a positive picture that reverberates with fans. The effect of marquee players stretches out past the limit, forming the view of the establishment in the bigger local area.

Chapter 4

The Chessboard Unveiled

"The Chessboard Uncovered" represents the complexities, procedures, and determined moves intrinsic in the realm of cricket barters, especially the Indian Chief Association (IPL) barters. The closeout room, similar to a chessboard, turns into the stage where establishment proprietors, mentors, and specialists participate in an essential game to gather the most considerable crews, contending with one another to get the best players and, thusly, secure T20 brilliance.

The chessboard allegory is especially adept while taking apart the elements of the shut offering stage, the underlying continues on this essential war zone. Groups submit fixed envelopes, hiding their offers for explicit players, making an air of mystery and interest. Similar as a chess player considering their initial ruse, establishments cautiously evaluate their choices, player valuations, and key needs prior to making their fixed offers. The shut offering stage establishes the vibe for the resulting fights on the chessboard, as groups disclose their underlying moves chasing a triumphant mix.

Progressing to the open offering stage is much the same as the midgame in a chess match, where the players adjust their methodologies in view of the developing elements of the board.

The chessboard, in this specific situation, is the closeout room where establishments decisively bid for players progressively. The open offering stage releases a whirlwind of moves, counter-moves, and key choices as groups vie for similar players. The recurring pattern of offers reflect the strategic moving on a chessboard, with establishments working out their moves in light of their rivals' activities.

The actual players address the chess pieces, each having one of a kind credits and jobs. Marquee players, the lords and sovereigns of this chessboard, convey the most noteworthy worth and impact. Establishments decisively position their marquee players, similar as strong chess pieces directing the progression of the game. The offering battles for marquee players become high-stakes conflicts, with groups decisively moving to outsmart their adversaries and secure the most sought after chess pieces.

The Option to Match (RTM) cards, an essential device presented in the IPL closeout, add one more layer to the chessboard. The RTM cards permit establishments to hold specific players from their past season by matching the most elevated bid in the closeout. This essential choice powers groups to expect their rivals' moves, similar as expecting an adversary's reaction to a chess move. The choice of when to play the RTM card turns into a critical part of the chessboard procedure, requiring premonition and the capacity to peruse the game.

The chessboard analogy stretches out to the essential breaks during the closeout, similar to the stops between chess moves where players mull over their subsequent stages. These breaks furnish establishments with a second to reconsider their techniques, talk with group the executives, and recalibrate their offering plans. The essential breaks are basic recesses in the speedy closeout climate, permitting groups to recover center, change their situations on the chessboard, and go with informed choices for the following offering stage.

Spending plan contemplations act as the limitations on this chessboard. Each establishment is designated a restricted spending plan, similar to the imperatives on the quantity of moves a chess player can make inside a set time period. The monetary discipline expected in the bartering room reflects the essential dynamic in chess, where players should advance their assets to outsmart rivals. Establishments decisively distribute their spending plan, gauging the worth of marquee players against the requirement for a reasonable crew.

The chessboard allegory likewise applies to the job of group proprietors, mentors, and planners as the grandmasters arranging the moves. The grandmasters on the IPL chessboard are the draftsmen of their group's fate, pursuing determined choices, expecting adversaries' moves, and decisively situating their pieces for greatest effect. The grandmasters should consider the drawn out vision, weighing prompt increases against future possibilities, similar as a chess player exploring through an intricate final stage.

The shut offering stage, much the same as the initial moves in a chess game, requires a profound comprehension of player valuations, economic situations, and the opposition. The underlying moves set the vibe for the resulting stages, directing the bearing of the closeout. Establishments decisively position themselves, assessing the qualities and shortcomings of their rivals, and taking very much considered actions that line up with their general methodology.

As the closeout advances, the chessboard turns into a milestone for key duels. Offering wars unfurl, suggestive of extreme chess matches where rivals participate in strategic trades. The players on the chessboard (marquee players and others) become the central marks of these fights, with establishments decisively offering to outsmart their opponents. The elements of market interest, combined with the limited assets of the compensation cap, add layers of intricacy to these essential fights.

The chessboard is likewise a material where startling moves and shocks can modify the direction of the game. Arising gifts, similar as flighty chess moves, bring a component of shock into the sale elements. Establishments should adjust rapidly, assessing the capability of these startling players and changing their techniques in like manner. The capacity to explore the unexpected turns on the chessboard is a demonstration of the strength and flexibility of the grandmasters.

The final plan in chess is a basic stage where players endeavor to combine their benefits and secure triumph. In the IPL closeout, the final stage is portrayed by essential dynamic in the last stages. Establishments should evaluate their left-over spending plan, address any holes in their crew, and take key actions to adjust their group arrangement. The final stage on the IPL chessboard requires a sensible harmony between obtaining headliners and filling explicit jobs inside spending plan imperatives.

The chessboard analogy stretches out past the bartering space to the genuine IPL season. When the crews are settled, the groups leave on an excursion where each match is out of here the bigger chessboard of the competition. The techniques executed during the closeout shape the group's playing XI, batting request, bowling revolutions, and field situations. The grandmasters proceed to plan all through the season, taking strategic actions in light of the developing elements of the competition.

The effect of the chessboard systems is obvious in the group's general execution, similar as the result of a chess game mirroring the viability of a player's moves. Groups that effectively explore the chessboard of the closeout, gather an even crew, and settle on key in-game choices are better situated for outcome in the IPL. The chessboard techniques are a nonstop string that runs from the closeout space to the cricket field, forming the predetermination of establishments in the T20 spectacle.

4.1 Franchise tactics in the auction room

Establishment strategies in the IPL sell off room are an enamoring mix of procedure, prescience, and flexibility, much the same as a chess match where each move is determined to get the best players inside the limitations of spending plans and group necessities. The closeout room changes into a strategic field, with establishment proprietors, mentors, and tacticians sending different strategies to outmaneuver their rivals, collect a triumphant crew, and explore the intricacies of player acquisitions.

The Shut Offering Stage fills in as the initial ruse in the sale room, where establishment strategies are first uncovered. This stage is described via fixed offers presented by groups for explicit players, covered in a demeanor of mystery. Establishments decisively assess the underlying player pool, survey their crew needs, and designate financial plans for vital participants. The shut offering stage turns into a urgent strategic moving ground where groups expect to get crucial players while sticking to monetary limitations. The initial strategies set the vibe for the resulting phases of the bartering, impacting the general technique and heading of each establishment.

The sending of Right to Match (RTM) cards is a strategic move that adds layers to establishment techniques in the bartering. These cards permit establishments to hold players from their past season by matching the most noteworthy bid in the bartering. The choice of when to play the RTM card turns into an essential thought, expecting establishments to evaluate the market worth of held players, expect to contend offers, and decisively use the RTM cards to keep up with crew coherence without surpassing monetary cutoff points. The RTM strategies include a sensitive harmony between holding center players and procuring new gifts, impacting the general piece of the group.

Spending plan contemplations assume a focal part in establishment strategies during the sale. Each group is dispensed a particular spending plan for player acquisitions, stressing the requirement for monetary discipline and key distribution of assets. Establishments should choose the amount of their financial plan to designate to marquee players, arising abilities, and explicit situations inside the crew. The monetary strategies include a sensitive difficult exercise — endeavoring to get effective players while guaranteeing there are adequate assets to construct a balanced and cutthroat group.

Vital breaks in the bartering room are likened to snapshots of consideration in a chess match, giving establishments a chance to rethink their strategies, talk with group the board, and change their offering plans.

These breaks in the speedy sale climate permit groups to recover, recalibrate their situations on the strategic chessboard, and settle on informed choices for the following offering stage. Vital breaks are a strategic rest, empowering establishments to remain on the ball and change their methodologies in light of the unfurling elements of the closeout.

The strategic moves of establishments strengthen during offering wars, which are vital duels where groups contend savagely for similar players. The chessboard wakes up with fast fire moves as establishments take part in strategic trades to outbid their opponents. The offering wars include a blend of hostility, tolerance, and determined navigation. Establishments decisively evaluate the qualities and shortcomings of their rivals, check player valuations, and adjust their strategies to get the ideal players inside monetary cutoff points. Offering wars become the cauldron where establishment techniques are scrutinized, and the strategic insight of groups is displayed.

The choice of marquee players addresses a significant stage in establishment strategies. Marquee players are the royal gems of the closeout, telling high valuations and filling in as the key parts of a group's technique. Establishments should choose whether to embrace a forceful methodology, getting marquee players at any expense, or to situate themselves for esteem acquisitions decisively. The strategic contemplations include evaluating the general crew needs, grasping the market elements, and adjusting the securing of marquee players to the group's drawn out vision and character.

Arising gifts, frequently alluded to as the surprisingly strong contenders of the bartering, assume a urgent part in establishment strategies. While marquee players draw at the center of attention, the essential incorporation of arising gifts is a strategic move that can deliver rich profits. Establishments should distinguish promising youthful players, measure their expected effect, and decisively bid to get these unlikely treasures. The strategic choice to put resources into arising gifts mirrors a forward-looking methodology, as these players can develop into key resources for the establishment throughout different seasons.

Vital designations during the sale include a round of mental strategies, impacting the offering elements and possibly disrupting rivals. Establishments decisively select players they may not really be keen on, making a redirection or raising the offering stakes for their opponents. The strategic utilization of designations means to make vulnerability, upset the plans of adversaries, and decisively position the assigning establishment for beneficial moves later in the closeout.

The utilization of examination and information driven experiences addresses a cutting edge feature of establishment strategies in the sale room. Establishments utilize analysts, investigators, and cricket specialists to do the math, assess player exhibitions, and reveal stowed away patterns.

The strategic utilization of information examination empowers establishments to pursue informed choices, recognize underestimated players, and decisively position themselves in the offering system. The reconciliation of information driven experiences into establishment strategies mirrors a contemporary way to deal with player acquisitions in the powerful scene of T20 cricket.

The Final plan in the sale room includes key dynamic in the last stages, similar as the finishing up moves of a chess match where players endeavor to merge their benefits and secure triumph. Establishments should decisively survey their leftover financial plan, address any holes in their crew, and take determined actions to finish their group sythesis. The strategic final stage requires a wise harmony between securing headliners and filling explicit jobs inside financial plan limitations, guaranteeing that the last crew lines up with the establishment's general technique.

The effect of establishment strategies in the sale room stretches out past the offering battles to shape the story of the whole IPL season. The choices made during the sale impact group arrangement, playing methodologies, and the general seriousness of establishments in the T20 event. Establishment strategies are not static; they advance in light of the changing elements of the sale, unforeseen turns, and the requirement for versatility. The capacity to explore the strategic complexities of the bartering room separates effective establishments, exhibiting their essential ability and premonition chasing after IPL magnificence.

4.2 Balancing star power with team cohesion

The fragile craft of offsetting star power with group union addresses a lasting test for establishments in the Indian Head Association (IPL). The T20 event, known for its high-profile acquisitions and marquee players, expects groups to strike an agreeable balance between elegant line-ups and the fundamental paste that ties a group together — union. This unpredictable equilibrium includes vital navigation, smart crew organization, and keen initiative to make a triumphant recipe that exploits individual splendor while cultivating a bound together camaraderie.

At the core of this difficult exercise is the essential choice of marquee players. These cricketing symbols, frequently venerated universally, bring their on-field ability as well as a critical off-field presence and attractiveness. Establishments decisively intend to get marquee players, perceiving the double effect they can have in the group's presentation and brand esteem. In any case, the test lies in guaranteeing that the star force of individual players doesn't eclipse the aggregate strength and solidarity of the group.

The determination of marquee players is a nuanced interaction that includes adjusting the group's essential goals to the properties and abilities of the headliners. While marquee players add energy, appeal, and game evolving skills, establishments should cautiously survey how these players fit into the group's general piece. The difficult exercise expects establishments to think about the singular splendor of marquee players as well as their similarity with the group's playing style, administration elements, and the jobs they are supposed to satisfy.

Finding some kind of harmony between star power and group union requires a more extensive point of view on crew organization. While marquee players rule the titles, the progress of an IPL group depends on the aggregate commitments of the whole crew. Establishments should cautiously gather a mix of experienced players, arising gifts, and utility players who can supplement the star power while adding profundity and equilibrium to the group. The strategic consideration of players who flourish in unambiguous jobs upgrades the general attachment of the crew.

Group attachment isn't exclusively subject to the headliners; it reaches out to the initiative elements inside the group. The arrangement of commanders and bad habit skippers assumes a crucial part in cultivating solidarity and coordination. Skippers are strategic geniuses on the field as well as pioneers who set the vibe for group culture, flexibility, and fellowship. Offsetting star power with group attachment expects establishments to choose pioneers who can saddle the qualities of individual players while making a common vision that joins the whole crew.

The Option to Match (RTM) cards, an essential device in the IPL closeout, acquaint an extra layer with the difficult exercise. Establishments, having held players from the past season, should decisively convey RTM cards to hold explicit players while exploring financial plan imperatives. The choice to utilize RTM cards includes gauging the worth of individual players against the more extensive crew necessities. Offsetting star power with group union in the RTM cycle expects establishments to pursue key decisions that upgrade the general seriousness and science of the crew.

The difficult exercise is maybe generally articulated during offering battles for marquee players in the closeout room. The extreme rivalry among establishments to get headliners frequently prompts expanded offers, extending group spending plans as far as possible. The test lies in keeping up with monetary discipline while likewise guaranteeing that the group gains the marquee players essential for an upper hand. Effective establishments display the capacity to explore offering wars in a calculated way, getting headliners at ideal valuations without compromising the general group organization.

The job of group proprietors and the executives becomes vital in directing the harmony between star power and group union. Proprietors, frequently confronted with the appeal of high-profile signings, should adjust their desires to the essential vision for the group.

The test lies in opposing the compulsion to seek after marquee players to the detriment of crew profundity and equilibrium. Proprietors who focus on long haul accomplishment over transient excitement add to a culture that values group union and supported seriousness.

The strategic utilization of uncapped players likewise assumes a critical part in the difficult exercise. Arising abilities, unrestricted by the heaviness of elevated requirements, can infuse essentialness into the crew while offering financially savvy commitments. Establishments that decisively recognize and sustain uncapped players figure out some kind of harmony between star power and group attachment. The combination of arising gifts supplements the marquee players, adding to a balanced crew that can adjust to the difficulties of a requesting T20 season.

Key crew revolutions and player the executives become vital in keeping up with the balance between star power and group attachment all through the IPL season. The persistent timetable, combined with player weakness and wounds, expects establishments to settle on wise choices on player turns. The difficult exercise includes giving sufficient rest to vital participants, guaranteeing the crew stays new, and giving chances to seat players to contribute seriously when called upon. Fruitful establishments show strategic sharpness in overseeing player responsibilities, safeguarding headliners' wellness while supporting the profundity of the crew.

The group culture and climate developed by establishments play a characterizing job in offsetting star power with group union. A positive and comprehensive group culture encourages a feeling of having a place and common perspective among players, rising above individual star status. Establishments that focus on a cooperative ethos, open correspondence, and an aggregate obligation to progress add to a climate where headliners consistently coordinate into the more extensive texture of the group.

Key instructing and uphold staff additionally add to the sensitive difficult exercise. Mentors should saddle the exceptional abilities of headliners while ingraining a group first mindset. The strategic direction given by instructing staff impacts playing procedures, individual jobs, and the general methodology of the group. Mentors who work out some kind of harmony between releasing the capability of headliners and encouraging group union make a triumphant recipe that rises above individual brightness.

The effect of offsetting star power with group union turns out to be generally evident during the pot of IPL matches. The on-field exhibitions, associations, and shared festivals mirror the progress of establishments in blending individual splendor with aggregate exertion. Groups that ace the difficult exercise display flexibility during testing circumstances, rally together during misfortunes, and grandstand a flexibility that stems from the integral qualities of headliners and group union.

The effect is additionally felt in the more extensive cricketing story, where establishments become images of vital keenness and manageable achievement. The difficult exercise is certainly not a one-time try however a continuous cycle that develops with each season. Effective establishments, throughout the long term, construct a heritage that exemplifies the sensitive balance between star power and group union. Their capacity to explore the intricacies of T20 cricket, pursue keen choices in the bartering room, and cultivate a triumphant culture highlights the getting through effect of a professional difficult exercise.

4.3 Navigating the challenge of player retention and release

The test of player maintenance and delivery in the Indian Chief Association (IPL) epitomizes a mind boggling and vital undertaking for establishments. The yearly sale fills in as the stage where groups should wisely explore the fragile equilibrium of holding central participants, delivering underperformers, and decisively remaking their crews. This mind boggling process includes a mix of execution examination, key premonition, and monetary contemplations to gather a serious group that lines up with the establishment's vision and goals.

Player maintenance is a foundation of crew the board in the IPL, permitting establishments to keep up with coherence and dependability by protecting a center gathering of players from the past season. The maintenance technique includes a cautious assessment of individual exhibitions, initiative characteristics, and the general effect of players in the group's prosperity. Establishments should figure out some kind of harmony between holding demonstrated entertainers and making adaptability in their crew to address regions that might require support.

The maintenance choices are impacted by a blend of cricketing insight and monetary contemplations. Establishments should evaluate the market worth of held players, taking into account their ongoing structure, influence in the group, and the interest for their administrations in the closeout. The monetary perspective presents a basic aspect, as establishments should streamline their financial plan while guaranteeing they hold players who offer the best benefit for cash and line up with the group's essential objectives.

The Option to Match (RTM) cards further entangle the maintenance system, presenting a component of vulnerability and key gamesmanship. Establishments should expect the moves of their rivals, check the possible offers for their held players, and decisively convey RTM cards to get key people. The RTM methodology expects establishments to evaluate the market elements, go with determined choices, and work out some kind of harmony between holding center players and expanding their monetary adaptability.

The maintenance interaction likewise includes contemplations past individual exhibitions, including the jobs and obligations every player satisfies inside the crew.

Establishments should assess the cooperative energy between held players, guaranteeing a balanced group structure that covers all features of the game. The test lies in distinguishing players who complete one another qualities, making a firm unit that can explore the different difficulties of the T20 design.

On the other hand, player discharge choices request a basic assessment of individual exhibitions, wellness levels, and the developing requirements of the group. Establishments face the difficult assignment of heading out in different directions from players who might have been important for the group's process however never again line up with the essential course. The delivery interaction requires a sensitive harmony between recognizing a player's previous commitments and pursuing realistic choices to upgrade the group's seriousness.

The delivery system includes a blend of execution measurements and crew prerequisites. Establishments should survey the measurable commitments of players, taking into account batting midpoints, bowling strike rates, and handling ability. In any case, the assessment goes past simple numbers, enveloping the intangibles like authority characteristics, flexibility, and the capacity to flourish under tension. The test is to work out some kind of harmony between regarding a player's heritage and going with choices that position the group for future achievement.

Vital prescience becomes foremost in player maintenance and delivery choices. Establishments should assess current exhibitions as well as undertaking the future direction of players. Arising gifts, who might not stand out in past seasons, present an essential chance for maintenance and improvement. Offsetting laid out stars with arising gifts adds to a balanced crew that can adjust to the developing elements of T20 cricket.

The difficult exercise stretches out to the allotment of abroad player openings. Establishments should decisively survey the effect and flexibility of their held abroad players, guaranteeing a wise blend of experienced campaigners and arising gifts. The test lies in improving the abroad spaces to handle an imposing playing XI while keeping up with adaptability for future closeouts. The abroad player technique turns into a significant component in the general maintenance and delivery math.

Player faithfulness and profound associations further entangle the dynamic interaction. Establishments frequently face the difficulty of whether to hold a cherished player with a solid fan following, regardless of whether their new exhibitions may not legitimize maintenance. The profound association among players and fans adds a layer of intricacy to the essential contemplations, as establishments should gauge the opinions of allies against the in field necessities of the group.

The planning of player maintenance and delivery declarations is an essential viewpoint that establishments cautiously consider. The grouping wherein establishments uncover their maintenance choices can impact the elements of the sale and set the vibe for their general technique. Early declarations might give lucidity and permit groups to decisively make arrangements for the closeout, while postponing choices can make a demeanor of tension and possibly influence the offering elements.

The monetary scene of the IPL acquaints a difficult aspect with player maintenance and delivery. Establishments work inside a compensation cap, requiring reasonable monetary administration to collect a serious crew inside monetary imperatives. The maintenance of marquee players frequently orders a huge piece of the spending plan, expecting establishments to settle on insightful choices on the distribution of assets to hold a harmony between star power and crew profundity.

The effect of player maintenance and delivery resounds past the sale room, forming the story of the forthcoming IPL season. Fans enthusiastically anticipate declarations, taking apart the held players and conjecturing on the essential bearing of their number one establishments. The choices made by groups add to the expectation and fervor encompassing the T20 party, making way for the recharged contentions and collusions that characterize each season.

The far reaching influences of player maintenance and delivery are felt all through the association, affecting the cutthroat equilibrium and stories of individual establishments. Effective maintenance systems add to a feeling of steadiness and personality inside a group, permitting players to expand on existing organizations and figure out their jobs inside the crew. On the other hand, canny delivery choices open up open doors for arising gifts and infuse new energy into groups, encouraging a feeling of restoration and flexibility.

The difficulties of player maintenance and delivery are not static; they advance with each season and are impacted by the always changing scene of T20 cricket. Establishments should consistently evaluate the presentation directions of players, adjust to arising patterns in the game, and decisively position themselves for supported achievement. The sensitive difficult exercise requires a mix of cricketing sharpness, key premonition, and a comprehension of the beat of the group and its fanbase.

Chapter 5

Emerging Talents and Surprise Picks

The Indian Head Association (IPL) isn't simply a phase for laid out cricketing lights; it likewise fills in as a favorable place for arising gifts and shock picks. In the midst of the sparkling cluster of global hotshots, the unheralded newbies and startling determinations frequently get everyone's attention. This powerful scene highlights the association's obligation to sustaining youthful ability, giving a stage to them to sparkle, and astounding cricket fans with new faces who become the heartbeat of the competition.

The development of youthful gifts in the IPL is a demonstration of the association's obligation to uncovering and sustaining promising cricketers. The competition's construction and the ethos of establishments underline the significance of mixing experience with youth. It is a feature where obscure gifts can change into commonly recognized names for the time being, making a permanent imprint on the cricketing scene.

Establishments, as they continued looking for progress, focus intently on exploring and preparing youthful abilities. The IPL closeout turns into a performance center of shocks, with establishments decisively focusing on promising uncapped players who have the possibility to have a tremendous effect. These arising gifts frequently rise up out of homegrown and Under-19 cricket, carrying with them a yearning to show what them can do on a great stage.

The unexpected picks in the sale are much the same as whole jewels ready to be cleaned. Establishments influence their exploring organizations and cricketing astuteness to distinguish players who could have gone unnoticed. The unconventionality of these determinations adds a component of energy to the sale procedures, with fans and specialists the same enthusiastically expecting the divulging of unlikely treasures who might actually change the direction of the competition.

The meaning of arising abilities in the IPL reaches out past their nearby effect on the field. These youthful players infuse newness into the association, testing the laid out request and implanting a feeling of unconventionality. Their boldness and richness reverberate with fans, making an interface that goes past insights. The development of an obscure ability or an unexpected pick adds a layer of narrating to the competition, where longshots become legends and add to the association's fables.

The IPL sell off is a venue of dreams for the vast majority arising gifts. The offering battles for uncapped players unfurl like holding stories, with establishments competing to get the administrations of the most encouraging young people. The unexpected picks frequently become the central marks of serious offering, mirroring the conviction that these players have the possibility to be major advantages. The closeout room turns into a phase where professions are sent off, and the predeterminations of youthful cricketers take a conclusive turn.

The IPL's obligation to supporting arising abilities is further clear in the playing XI elements during the competition. Establishments perceive the benefit of giving open doors to youthful players, incorporating them into the crew close by laid out stars. The mix of youth and experience establishes an agreeable group climate, cultivating mentorship and working with the consistent change of arising gifts into the expert field.

The unexpected picks additionally add to the association's story by testing assumptions and challenging generalizations. Players who might not have had the focus on them in the customary cricketing structure out of nowhere end up push into the spotlight. The IPL turns into a phase where whimsical gifts, with one of a kind abilities and playing styles, are commended for their distinction. Shock picks frequently carry variety to the association, mirroring the worldwide idea of the game and displaying cricket's capacity to embrace ability from different cricketing scenes.

The excursion of arising abilities in the IPL isn't without its difficulties. The change from homegrown or age-bunch cricket to the high-pressure climate of the IPL requests strength, versatility, and a speedy expectation to learn and adapt. Youthful players face the overwhelming errand of going up against worldwide stalwarts, and their exhibitions under the splendid lights of the IPL are investigated by fans, savants, and selectors the same. The association turns into a pot where arising gifts are produced through the cauldron of high-stakes experiences.

The effect of arising gifts goes past the prompt season. Fruitful exhibitions in the IPL frequently open ways to worldwide open doors, with champion players acquiring public group call-ups. The association fills in as an entryway for youthful cricketers to declare their appearance on the worldwide stage, and shock picks who sparkle in the IPL become piece of the bigger story of cricketing examples of overcoming adversity.

Shock picks additionally feature the essential astuteness of establishment think tanks. The capacity to recognize underestimated or neglected players, survey their possible effect, and decisively bid for them is a demonstration of the premonition and exploring abilities of establishments. The unexpected picks become vital weapons, with establishments planning to get effective players at ideal valuations, frequently jumbling assumptions and outsmarting their opponents in the sale room.

The IPL closeout isn't simply about gaining marquee players; about building a decent crew can climate the afflictions of a T20 competition. Establishments perceive the requirement for profundity and flexibility in their crews, and arising gifts assume a crucial part in giving those credits. Shock picks frequently satisfy explicit jobs inside the crew, whether as hard-hitting finishers, successful bowlers, or coordinated defenders, adding to the general equilibrium of the group.

The unexpected picks additionally challenge the laid out standards of player valuation. While marquee players order robust sticker prices, the unexpected picks frequently offer extraordinary benefit for cash. Establishments that distinguish and get these underestimated pearls accomplish an upper hand, as they get players fit for conveying exhibitions that far surpass their bartering cost. The capacity to find stowed away fortunes in the closeout room turns into a sign of fruitful establishments.

The stories of arising gifts and amaze picks entwine with the more extensive topic of democratizing cricketing valuable open doors. The IPL's comprehensive construction gives a stage to cricketers from different foundations, independent of their cricketing family, to feature their abilities. The association turns into a mixture where ability, regardless of its starting point, is perceived, celebrated, and allowed the opportunity to prosper. This democratization of chances lines up with the advancing ethos of current cricket, where meritocracy overshadows conventional ordered progressions.

The effect of arising gifts and shock picks isn't restricted to on-handle exhibitions; it reaches out to the fan insight. The flightiness presented by these players adds a component of interest to the competition. Fans revel in seeing the fleeting ascent of youthful cricketers, rooting for the longshots who surprise everyone and leave an imprint on the stupendous stage. The rise of shock picks turns into a common story that joins fans across different foundations, encouraging a feeling of aggregate festival.

Establishments that effectively coordinate arising abilities into their crews add to the association's tradition of supporting cricketing ability. The capacity to establish a helpful climate for youthful players to flourish, furnishing them with mentorship, and cultivating a culture of ceaseless learning is a sign of fruitful establishments. The effect of these arising gifts reaches out past individual exhibitions; it shapes the ethos of the establishment and impacts the association's more extensive account.

The IPL closeout, with its accentuation on shock picks and arising gifts, reflects the substance of T20 cricket — a configuration that commends dynamism, development, and the intrepid quest for progress. The association's obligation to giving a stage to unheralded cricketers lines up with the ethos of T20 cricket, where the game's customary shows are tested, and individual brightness frequently outweighs everything else. The IPL turns into a microcosm of the developing cricketing scene, where shock picks and arising gifts are essential to the association's charm and its capacity to dazzle crowds around the world.

5.1 Unearthing hidden gems in the auction

The Indian Chief Association (IPL) closeout isn't just an exhibition of high-stakes offering for laid out stars; it is an essential front line where establishments mean to uncover unexpected, yet invaluable treasures — those unheralded players whose potential may not be promptly clear yet can fundamentally influence the course of the competition. Uncovering unlikely treasures in the sale requires a sharp eye for ability, canny exploring organizations, and the capacity to unravel the natural worth that goes past the player's standing or past exhibitions.

The elements of the IPL sell off request establishments to go past the conspicuous decisions and dive into the pool of uncapped and arising players. These whole jewels address a chance for groups to get effective players at moderately lower costs, contributing not exclusively to the group's prompt achievement yet in addition to its drawn out maintainability. The quest for unlikely treasures mirrors the substance of the IPL as an association that values development, key intuition, and the capacity to detect potential where others may not.

The exploring system turns into a basic forerunner to uncovering unlikely treasures in the closeout. Establishments concentrate on building complete exploring networks that length homegrown contests, age-bunch competitions, and less popular cricketing circuits.

The goal is to distinguish players with one of a kind abilities, undiscovered capacity, and the craving to leave an imprint on the fantastic phase of the IPL. Exploring reports, measurable examinations, and firsthand evaluations add to the production of a waitlist of players who could be the unlikely treasures in the sale.

The essential utilization of examination assumes a critical part in the ID of unlikely treasures. Establishments utilize analysts, information investigators, and cricket specialists to do the math, evaluate player exhibitions, and reveal patterns that may not be promptly clear. The information driven approach empowers groups to go past emotional assessments and settle on informed choices in view of true measurements. Unlikely treasures frequently rise up out of factual exceptions, and establishments that influence examination gain a strategic advantage in the mission for underestimated ability.

The closeout room turns into a performance center of shocks when establishments reveal their procedures to get unexpected, yet invaluable treasures. These players are frequently brought into the offering system at vital minutes, surprising adversaries and possibly prompting extraordinary offering wars. The unconventionality related with unexpected, yet invaluable treasures adds a component of energy to the closeout, as establishments mean to get high-influence players at costs that may not mirror their actual worth.

The uncapped player classification turns into an especially fruitful ground for uncovering unlikely treasures. These players, who might not have the worldwide openness or acknowledgment, convey a feeling of secret and interest. Establishments perceive the potential in uncapped players who have succeeded in home-grown rivalries, and the essential offering for these unlikely treasures turns into a back-and-forth where groups strive to get promising gifts before their actual worth is generally recognized.

The offering methodology for unexpected, yet invaluable treasures includes a fragile harmony among hostility and monetary reasonability. Establishments should be emphatic in chasing after players they recognize as likely major advantages, however they likewise need to practice limitation to try not to overextend their spending plans. The craft of getting unlikely treasures lies in essential offering — entering the conflict at the lucky second, checking the opposition, and making very much determined offers that mirror the apparent worth of the player.

The Option to Match (RTM) cards, a one of a kind element in the IPL sell off, add one more layer to the quest for unlikely treasures. Establishments have the choice to hold explicit players from their past crews by matching the most elevated bid made by different groups. The essential utilization of RTM cards expects establishments to evaluate the market worth of held players and decisively convey the cards for players they think about unexpected, yet invaluable treasures. The RTM strategies become an essential chess game, with establishments expecting to hold significant players without surpassing monetary requirements.

The effect of unexpected, yet invaluable treasures reaches out past their financial worth; it shapes the account of the IPL season. Players who were generally obscure before the sale out of nowhere end up push into the spotlight, bearing liabilities and becoming indispensable pieces of their separate groups. The progress of unlikely treasures reverberates with fans, as these players epitomize the longshot soul and add to the unusualness that makes T20 cricket so charming.

The job of group the executives and training staff becomes essential in opening the capability of unlikely treasures. These players frequently require sustaining, direction, and amazing open doors to exhibit their capacities. Fruitful establishments establish a climate where unlikely treasures can prosper, giving them the help, mentorship, and strategic bits of knowledge expected to make a consistent progress to the high-pressure field of the IPL.

The versatility of unlikely treasures turns into a critical consider their prosperity. These players might not have the worldwide openness or experience of playing in high-profile associations, setting their acclimation to the expectations of the IPL a critical test. Establishments that perceive and upgrade the flexibility of unlikely treasures, assisting them with developing as adaptable supporters of the group's prosperity, open the genuine capability of these players.

The effect of unlikely treasures isn't limited to a solitary IPL season; it frequently adds to the getting through progress and tradition of establishments. Players who were once unlikely treasures turned into the foundations of groups, advancing into pioneers and guides for the up and coming age of arising gifts. The capacity of establishments to reliably distinguish and support unexpected, yet invaluable treasures mirrors a practical way to deal with crew building and a guarantee to long haul achievement.

Unexpected, yet invaluable treasures likewise challenge the traditional thoughts of player valuation. While marquee players order significant sticker prices, unexpected, yet invaluable treasures frequently offer remarkable benefit for cash. The capacity to get significant players at somewhat lower costs permits establishments to enhance their financial plans, making a balanced crew that consolidates star power with profundity. The essential quest for unlikely treasures mirrors a monetary judiciousness that adds to the general intensity of establishments.

The effect of unexpected, yet invaluable treasures isn't restricted to the field of play; it reaches out to the more extensive cricketing biological system. The examples of overcoming adversity of players who were once unexpected, yet invaluable treasures move another age of cricketers, reaffirming the conviction that ability, assurance, and the ideal time can prompt accomplishment on the most excellent stages. The rise of unlikely treasures turns into a story string in the bigger embroidery of the IPL, adding layers of narrating and adding to the association's character.

The quest for unlikely treasures in the IPL sell off mirrors the substance of T20 cricket — an organization that praises development, versatility, and the unforeseen. Establishments that embrace the test of uncovering unexpected, yet invaluable treasures encapsulate the soul of the association, where vital astuteness and the capacity to detect potential characterize achievement. The quest for unlikely treasures is a continuous undertaking that mirrors the consistently developing nature of the IPL, where the mission for underestimated ability is as integral to the association's appeal as the exhibitions of laid out stars.

5.2 The role of uncapped players in team strategy

The job of uncapped players in the technique of Indian Head Association (IPL) groups is a dynamic and complex viewpoint that essentially impacts the organization, elements, and progress of the crews. Uncapped players, frequently youthful and moderately obscure on the worldwide stage, assume a significant part in group technique, contributing with their abilities on the field as well as impacting different features of the group's general methodology. The essential organization of uncapped players includes a cautious harmony between supporting youthful ability, adding profundity to the crew, and boosting the group's likely inside the imperatives of the IPL biological system.

One of the essential jobs of uncapped players in group procedure is to give a new point of view and imbuement of energy into the crew. Youthful and energetic, uncapped players carry a craving to show what them can do at the most significant level. This yearning converts into an upper hand and a readiness to face challenges, qualities that can be significant in the quick moving and capricious climate of T20 cricket. Establishments decisively select uncapped players who line up with their group culture and playing reasoning, guaranteeing that the imbuement of youthful ability supplements the general procedure.

The strategic sending of uncapped players includes recognizing explicit jobs inside the crew where these players can make significant commitments. Uncapped players are frequently chosen for their specialization specifically abilities, whether it be unstable batting, wicket-taking bowling, or uncommon handling. Establishments decisively coordinate uncapped players into the playing XI in light of the necessities of each match, the qualities of the resistance, and the playing conditions. The capacity to use uncapped players decisively adds adaptability and versatility to group systems.

Uncapped players likewise assume a critical part in giving crew profundity, particularly taking into account the thorough and requesting timetable of the IPL. With consecutive matches and the potential for wounds, establishments decisively deal with their player assets by having a pool of skilled uncapped players prepared to step in when required. The seat strength, frequently containing uncapped players, turns into an essential resource for groups, permitting them to keep an elevated degree of seriousness all through the competition.

The IPL sell off is a stage where establishments effectively look for uncapped players who have the possibility to be huge advantages. The offering battles for uncapped gifts become vital fights where establishments, furnished with their exploring reports and key goals, strive to get players who can give an upper hand. The capacity to recognize underestimated uncapped players and secure them at ideal costs turns into a demonstration of the essential discernment of group proprietors, the executives, and scouts.

The Option to Match (RTM) cards further intensify the essential meaning of uncapped players. Establishments should choose when and how to send RTM cards for explicit players they wish to hold from the past season. The RTM methodology includes evaluating the market elements, measuring the possible offers for held players, and decisively sending the cards to amplify the crew's general strength. The choice to utilize RTM cards for uncapped players adds a layer of intricacy to group procedure, requiring a fragile harmony among progression and versatility.

The turn of events and sustaining of uncapped players are vital parts of group technique in the IPL. Establishments put resources into ability improvement programs, mentorship drives, and instructional courses to prepare uncapped players and set them up for the afflictions of T20 cricket. The essential vision incorporates quick commitments as well as the drawn out improvement of players who can become mainstays of the group in ensuing seasons. Effective establishments establish a climate that cultivates the development and development of uncapped players, guaranteeing a nonstop pipeline of ability.

Vital revolutions and match-explicit determinations further feature the job of uncapped players in group methodology. Establishments perceive that various players might succeed in unambiguous circumstances or against specific adversaries.

The strategic utilization of uncapped players permits groups to fit their playing XI to take advantage of resistance shortcomings, adjust to shifting playing surfaces, and profit by the assorted ranges of abilities inside the crew. The essential adaptability presented by uncapped players improves a group's capacity to explore the complexities of the competition.

Uncapped players frequently wind up push into essential jobs over the span of the IPL season, giving establishments chances to uncover unexpected, yet invaluable treasures. The capacity to recognize and gain by the capability of uncapped players turns into a distinctive variable for effective groups. Establishments that exhibit trust in their uncapped players, giving them valuable open doors in pressure circumstances, frequently receive benefits as these players adapt to the situation and contribute essentially to the group's prosperity.

The eccentricism related with uncapped players turns into an essential resource in itself. Rivals might have restricted data about the playing styles, qualities, and shortcomings of uncapped players, adding a component of shock to group techniques.

Establishments decisively convey uncapped players to take advantage of this unusualness, putting adversaries on the back foot and driving them to adjust on the fly. The essential utilization of vulnerability turns into a strategic benefit for groups ready to back their uncapped gifts.

The improvement of uncapped players additionally lines up with the more extensive cricketing ethos of sustaining neighborhood ability and adding to the development of the game in the district. Establishments perceive the significance of interfacing with the nearby fanbase and making a feeling of personality. Uncapped players, frequently rising up out of homegrown cricket or provincial foundations, become agents of the nearby cricketing environment. Their prosperity reverberates with fans, encouraging a more profound association between the group and the local area.

Key crew sythesis includes a sensitive harmony between star power and the mixture of uncapped players. While marquee players give the star remainder and global experience, uncapped players add profundity, energy, and a feeling of appeal to the crew. The essential mix of laid out stars and uncapped gifts makes a powerful group culture where players gain from one another, challenge one another, and on the whole take a stab at progress. The quest for this equilibrium is an essential basic for establishments going for the gold in the IPL.

The developing idea of T20 cricket, portrayed by advancements, striking techniques, and dynamic interactivity, lines up with the consideration of uncapped players in group methodologies. The configuration's accentuation on flexibility and genius tracks down a characteristic fit in the essential utilization of youthful, fiery, and less-unsurprising gifts. Uncapped players, unrestricted by the heaviness of assumptions, frequently carry a dauntless and imaginative way to deal with their game, adding to the essential dynamic quality of groups in the IPL.

The job of uncapped players reaches out past on-field commitments; it includes their effect in group culture, kinship, and solidarity. Uncapped players, frequently manufacturing their vocations in the pot of homegrown cricket, bring a modesty and craving that can emphatically influence group elements. Their excursion to the IPL addresses a fantasy understood, and the essential combination of uncapped players cultivates an aggregate feeling of direction and shared responsibility inside the crew.

5.3 Stories of underdog players making it big through the auction

The Indian Chief Association (IPL) has turned into a cauldron for cricketing dreams, where longshot players, frequently unheralded and disregarded, script convincing accounts of versatility, assurance, and win. These stories of longshot players becoming wildly successful through the IPL closeout resound with fans, adding a profound and moving layer to the competition's story.

The closeout room, with its high-stakes offering wars and vital moves, turns into the stage where uncelebrated yet truly great individuals arise, oppose chances, and engraving their names in the archives of T20 cricket history.

One of the characterizing elements of the IPL closeout is its ability to transform obscure players into mind-blowing phenomenons. These longshot players, frequently coming from contemporary cricketing foundations or less popular homegrown circuits, end up push into the spotlight as establishments perceive their undiscovered possibility. The flightiness of the sale interaction, with its accentuation on essential offering and shock picks, makes a rich ground for longshot stories to unfurl.

The excursion of longshot players in the IPL frequently starts with their consideration in the sale pool. These players might not have the worldwide qualifications or the acknowledgment that goes with laid out stars, yet they convey a deep yearning to exhibit their abilities on the fabulous stage. The sale turns into a stage where their cricketing predeterminations take an unequivocal turn, and establishments, furnished with exploring reports and key dreams, become the guardians of these players' fantasies.

Offering battles for dark horse players are a demonstration of the conviction that establishments have in their true capacity. The closeout room changes into a theater where groups, each with its essential targets and player inclinations, participate in extraordinary fights to get the administrations of players who could have been neglected in traditional cricketing circuits. The taking off bid sums for longshot players reflect their prompt effect as well as the commitment of future achievement that establishments mean to outfit.

The tales of longshot players becoming famous through the IPL closeout frequently imply key reasoning and potentially dangerous courses of action by establishments. These players might not have the factual benchmarks or the global openness that normally drive high offers, however insightful group the executives perceives the intangibles — character, versatility, and the yearning to succeed —

that can lift dark horse players into match-victors. The capacity of establishments to recognize underestimated gifts and decisively bid for them turns into a sign of fruitful group the board.

One of the most commended parts of the IPL is the democratization of chances, where longshot players from different cricketing foundations and age bunches wind up in a similar closeout pool as laid out stars. The sale turns into a level battleground where ability outweighs notoriety, and dark horse players get the opportunity to grandstand their abilities close by global stalwarts. This inclusivity adds to the lavishness and variety of the association's woven artwork.

The Option to Match (RTM) cards add a captivating layer to the dark horse story in the IPL. Establishments, perceiving the capability of dark horse players they might have supported in past seasons, decisively send RTM cards to hold these abilities. The RTM cycle includes an essential chess game, with groups measuring the market elements, foreseeing rival offers, and decisively using their cards to get dark horse players at ideal costs. The maintenance of longshot players through RTM cards adds coherence to their excursions, permitting them to expand on their past triumphs and further add to their establishments.

The effect of dark horse players isn't restricted to their singular exhibitions; it stretches out to the aggregate soul of the groups they address. Dark horse players, frequently with a highlight demonstrate, carry an infectious enthusiasm to the crew. Their processes reverberate with the dark horse soul — the capacity to defeat difficulties, blow some minds, and jump all over chances when they emerge. The longshot story turns into a wellspring of motivation for the whole group, cultivating an aggregate conviction that rises above individual accomplishments.

The examples of overcoming adversity of dark horse players in the IPL frequently include advancement seasons where they outflank assumptions and become critical gear-teeth in their group's prosperity. These players, when thought about exceptions, change into key parts of their crews, displaying their abilities and contributing game dominating exhibitions. The flightiness and intensity of the T20 design give the best material to dark horse players to flourish and make a permanent imprint.

The dark horse story acquires further reverberation when longshot players succeed in high-pressure circumstances, for example, knockout matches or finals. Their capacity to adapt to the situation, convey under extraordinary examination, and assume essential parts in extremely important occasions of the competition adds layers of show and feeling to their accounts. The longshot players, frequently with a background marked by confronting misfortune, become the legends who lead their groups to brilliance.

The effect of dark horse players stretches out past the limits of the cricket field; it saturates the fanbase and catches the aggregate creative mind of cricket aficionados. Fans, attracted to the credibility and appeal of longshot stories, rally behind these players, transforming them into clique figures. The dark horse players become images of trust, encapsulating the idea that fantasies can be acknowledged through difficult work, determination, and the perfect time. The close to home association between longshot players and fans makes a special bond that adds a persevering through aspect to the IPL experience.

The dark horse stories in the IPL likewise add to the bigger story of cricket as a game that celebrates ability, regardless of its starting point.

The association turns into a blend where players from different cricketing scenes, whether unassuming communities, less popular cricketing circuits, or arising cricketing countries, get an equivalent opportunity to exhibit their capacities. The longshot story supports that ability is general, and the IPL turns into a stage where players from fluctuated foundations can sparkle.

While the IPL has seen the fleeting ascent of dark horse players, their prosperity is in many cases a finish of long stretches of difficult work, diligence, and an excursion through the positions of homegrown and age-bunch cricket. The association gives a zenith of these endeavors, offering a stage for longshot players to exhibit their abilities on the fantastic stage. Their processes act as a wake up call of the more extensive cricketing biological system, where ability is sustained in the cauldron of homegrown contests and territorial foundations.

The IPL closeout, with its focus on dark horse players, likewise represents the association's obligation to encouraging ability and making a pathway for youthful cricketers to enter the expert field. The exploring organizations of establishments, frequently traversing different cricketing scenes, effectively look for players who might not have had the open door to exhibit their gifts on a public or global stage. The sale turns into a door for dark horse players to break into the major association and satisfy their cricketing desires.

The narratives of longshot players becoming showbiz royalty through the IPL sell off highlight the association's more extensive effect on the worldwide cricketing scene. The progress of these players rises above the limits of the competition, impacting the impression of T20 cricket as a configuration that gives equivalent open doors to players to feature their abilities. The IPL turns into a signal for hopeful cricketers around the world, propelling them to seek after their fantasies and trust in the chance of making progress on the great stage.

Chapter 6

Team Dynamics and Chemistry

Group elements and science are the immaterial yet significant components that can characterize the achievement or disappointment of a cricket crew in the Indian Head Association (IPL). In a configuration as unique and quick moving as T20 cricket, where individual splendor frequently becomes the overwhelming focus, the capacity of a group to work as a durable unit becomes central. The blend of different gifts, the producing areas of strength for of bonds, and the foundation of a common group culture add to the complicated embroidery of group elements in the IPL.

At the core of successful group elements is the choice interaction, especially during the IPL closeout. Establishments should not just gather a crew with an equilibrium of ranges of abilities yet additionally think about the similarity of players regarding playing styles, characters, and jobs inside the group. The closeout room turns into an essential landmark where establishments settle on choices that will shape the group elements for the whole season.

The marquee signings frequently set the vibe for a group's elements. Establishments focus on getting headliners who bring individual brightness as well as act as possible impetuses for group attachment. The essential obtaining of marquee players includes contemplations past their on-field exhibitions; establishments evaluate their initiative characteristics, group ethos, and capacity to add to a positive group culture.

The structure of a group in the IPL is a fragile harmony between laid out stars and arising gifts, each adding to the group elements in exceptional ways. While marquee players give the star power and experience, uncapped or longshot players bring energy, hunger, and a feeling of unusualness. Effective group elements rely on the capacity to incorporate these different components into a firm unit, where every player grasps their job and embraces the aggregate goal.

Initiative assumes an essential part in forming group elements. The chief, frequently the essence of the establishment, establishes the vibe for the group both on and off the field. The skipper's capacity to move, rouse, and encourage a positive group culture impacts the elements inside the crew. A commander's essential discernment, man-the board abilities, and the ability to draw out the best in every player contribute fundamentally to the general group elements.

Training staff likewise assume an essential part in molding group elements. The care staff, including mentors, guides, and examiners, add to the improvement of a firm group culture. Their job reaches out past specialized training; they become facilitators of group holding, correspondence, and the generally mental prosperity of players. Establishments that put resources into a vigorous care staff frequently receive the benefits concerning further developed group elements.

Group elements in the IPL are not entirely settled by on-field exhibitions; they stretch out to off-handle connections, group exercises, and the formation of a helpful group climate. Establishments coordinate group building works out, holding meetings, and off-field exercises to encourage fellowship among players. These drives add to the improvement of trust, understanding, and a common feeling of direction inside the group.

Correspondence is a key part of compelling group elements. The capacity of players and training staff to convey straightforwardly, truly, and valuably is imperative for tending to difficulties, settling clashes, and building a culture of common regard. Establishments that focus on straightforward correspondence establish a climate where players feel appreciated, esteemed, and put resources into the group's aggregate achievement.

In an association as different as the IPL, where players from various nations, societies, and cricketing foundations meet up, the job of group elements turns out to be much more articulated. Establishments should explore phonetic and social contrasts, cultivating a comprehensive climate where players from different foundations feel happy with communicating their thoughts. The festival of variety turns into a strength that enhances the group's elements instead of a possible wellspring of division.

The group elements are additionally impacted by the presence of notable players who rise above public limits. The IPL, frequently alluded to as a "cricketing festival," unites worldwide cricketing geniuses who combine efforts with neighborhood gifts. The mixture of worldwide and homegrown players, each bringing their remarkable assets and points of view, adds to the cosmopolitan idea of group elements in the IPL.

The test for establishments lies in consistently coordinating these different components into a firm unit. Social responsiveness, inclusivity, and a proactive way to deal with group holding become fundamental parts of dealing with a group with a worldwide sythesis. Effective establishments influence this variety as a competitive edge, empowering diverse communications and making a mixture of cricketing encounters.

The group elements in the IPL are not static; they develop throughout the competition in view of exhibitions, encounters, and outside factors. Establishments should be versatile and receptive to changes in structure, wounds, and unexpected difficulties. The capacity to recalibrate group elements in light of developing conditions is a sign of effective IPL crusades.

One of the principal traits of fruitful group elements is the production of a solid group culture. A positive group culture cultivates a feeling of having a place, responsibility, and versatility inside the crew. The development of a common ethos, values, and objectives turns into a directing power that rises above individual exhibitions and outer tensions. Establishments that put resources into building a strong group culture frequently find that it turns into a bedrock for supported achievement.

The IPL's requesting plan, with consecutive matches and incessant travel, puts extra weight on players truly and intellectually. Powerful group elements incorporate arrangements for player prosperity, rest and recuperation methodologies, and emotional well-being support. Establishments that focus on player government assistance contribute not exclusively to individual exhibitions yet in addition to the general flexibility and union of the group.

The group elements are especially clear during high-pressure minutes in matches, like close gets done or vital knockout experiences. The capacity of a group to remain formed, rally together, and execute under tension mirrors the strength of its elements. Establishments that develop a culture of versatility and a never-say-bite the dust mentality frequently arise as imposing rivals in the IPL.

The job of group elements in player maintenance is an essential thought for establishments. Effective groups frequently plan to hold a center gathering of players, encouraging coherence and solidness inside the crew. The maintenance methodology includes evaluating on-field exhibitions as well as thinking about the effect of players in group elements, administration, and the general group culture.

Interestingly, the IPL closeout turns into a chance for establishments to reshape their groups and present new elements. The essential securing of players includes contemplations past individual insights; establishments evaluate the expected effect of new signings in group science, playing mixes, and generally elements. The sale turns into a stage for groups to support their assets, address shortcomings, and implant new energy into their crews.

The IPL's configuration of player barters, with its dynamic offering process and the component of shock, adds an extra layer to group elements. The sale room turns into a microcosm of the essential fights that unfurl on the cricket field. Establishments should explore financial plan imperatives, contending offers, and the flightiness of player valuations to gather a crew that lines up with their essential vision.

Key reasoning is vital in the sale room, with establishments planning pre-sell off plans, recognizing objective players, and adjusting to the liquid idea of offering wars. The choices made during the sale resound all through the season, affecting group elements, playing blends, and the general seriousness of the crew. Fruitful establishments influence the sale as an essential device to create groups that are ability loaded as well as decisively adjusted.

The effect of group elements is maybe generally obvious during the IPL end of the season games and finals, where the tension arrives at its apex. Groups that have areas of strength for developed elements all through the season frequently find an additional stuff in these high-stakes experiences. The capacity to work as a strong unit, support each other under tension, and execute well thought out courses of action turns into the differentiator in the mission for the IPL prize.

The dark horse story, a repetitive subject in the IPL, adds a fascinating layer to group elements. Groups with a blend of laid out stars and dark horse players frequently track down that the yearning, excitement, and unusualness brought by the longshots contribute decidedly to group elements. The dark horse players, spurred to show what them can do on the enormous stage, add a unique component to group science and frequently become impetuses for progress.

6.1 The importance of team chemistry in T20 cricket

Group science in T20 cricket is a nuanced and basic component that goes past individual exhibitions and ranges of abilities. The briefest configuration of the game requests an extraordinary arrangement of abilities, flexibility, and an aggregate comprehension among colleagues to explore the speedy, high-pressure situations that characterize T20 cricket. The significance of group science in this organization isn't just clear in on-field associations yet in addition in the essential navigation, correspondence, and in general brotherhood that shapes a fruitful T20 group.

At the center of group science in T20 cricket is the idea of organizations. In contrast to longer organizations of the game, where time is in many cases on the batting group, T20 cricket requires quick and significant coordinated efforts between batsmen. Openers, specifically, assume a urgent part in establishing the vibe for the innings. The science between opening accomplices includes a profound comprehension of one another's playing styles, assets, and favored scoring zones. The capacity to turn the strike, convey successfully, and complete one another game becomes indispensable to laying out a strong groundwork.

The science between batsmen reaches out to the center request, where the capacity to construct organizations turns out to be considerably more critical. T20 cricket frequently witnesses fast wickets, and the center request batsmen must flawlessly adjust to the circumstance, turn the strike, and send off counter-assaults when required. Group science in the batting unit includes a mutual perspective of jobs, obligations, and the capacity to help each other in different match circumstances. Effective T20 groups exhibit a batting setup that works as a durable unit instead of an assortment of individual gifts.

Bowling associations are similarly imperative in T20 cricket, where bowlers should work pair to apply pressure, take wickets, and control the scoring rate. The science between new-ball bowlers, spinners, and passing overs experts turns into an essential resource for groups. Bowlers should complete one another qualities, adjust to changing match conditions, and execute all around facilitated plans to ruin resistance batsmen. Group science in the bowling division includes shared correspondence, field positions, and a comprehension of every bowler's favored lengths and varieties.

The job of all-rounders adds one more layer to group science in T20 cricket. These players contribute with both bat and ball, and their presence improves the group's adaptability and vital choices. The science between all-rounders and expert players includes a comprehension of when to speed up the scoring rate, when to secure the innings, and how to supplement the bowling assault. Fruitful T20 groups influence the flexibility, everything being equal, to make a decent and versatile unit.

Key decision-production in T20 cricket is vigorously impacted by group science. Skippers, mentors, and care staff should establish a climate where players feel happy with communicating their thoughts, giving info, and taking part in strategic conversations. The science between the initiative gathering and players is pivotal for adjusting the group's essential vision, encouraging a culture of cooperation, and pursuing continuous choices during matches. Fruitful T20 groups frequently feature a consistent reconciliation of key sharpness and compelling correspondence.

The significance of group science in T20 cricket is complemented by the organization's inborn eccentricism. Matches can swing decisively inside a couple of overs, and the capacity of a group to remain made, convey really, and rally together during testing minutes turns into a characterizing factor. Group science adds to an aggregate strength that empowers groups to return from difficulties, gain from encounters, and keep an uplifting perspective even in high-pressure circumstances.

In T20 cricket, where force is a short lived and valuable ware, group science assumes a significant part in making a positive environment inside the crew. The science between players, instructing staff, and backing work force adds to a durable group culture that values common regard, trust, and a common obligation to progress. Effective T20 groups frequently show a feeling of brotherhood that stretches out past on-field exhibitions and adds to an amicable group climate.

The elements of group science are likewise obvious in the craft of handling, an essential part of T20 cricket. Lithe and ready defenders, facilitated handling situations, and viable correspondence between players add to a group's general handling ability. The science between defenders, particularly in high-pressure circumstances, upgrades a group's capacity to set out run-out open doors, impact excusals, and apply strain on resistance batsmen.

The T20 design puts a top notch on versatility, and group science turns into an impetus for successful transformation. Establishments in T20 associations like the Indian Head Association (IPL) frequently highlight players from various cricketing foundations, identities, and societies. The capacity to absorb different gifts into a durable unit mirrors the strength of group science. Fruitful T20 groups gain by this variety, utilizing the extraordinary qualities of every player to make a balanced and versatile crew.

Powerful correspondence is a key part of group science in T20 cricket. The speedy idea of the organization requests fast navigation, moment responses, and clear correspondence on the field. The science between defenders, bowlers, and the wicketkeeper includes consistent correspondence to facilitate handling arrangements, set going after or guarded fields, and convey vital experiences. Groups that focus on open and compelling correspondence cultivate a climate where players feel enabled to contribute their points of view.

The impact of group science stretches out to the changing area environment, a space where players re-energize, plan, and ponder their exhibitions. The science among players and the instructing staff adds to a positive and strong climate that supports individual gifts and cultivates aggregate development. Fruitful T20 groups focus on a changing area culture that joins force on the field with fellowship off the field.

The T20 design additionally delivers the idea of group elements regarding player turns and the use of crew profundity. Establishments in T20 associations frequently have huge crews with a blend of experienced players and arising gifts. The science between players, particularly the people who may not be in the beginning XI for each match, is vital for keeping a solid group culture. The capacity to pivot players decisively, give potential open doors to the whole crew, and guarantee that each part feels esteemed adds to a good group dynamic.

The closeout cycle, a novel part of T20 associations like the IPL, adds one more layer to group science. Establishments should explore the bartering room in a calculated way, pursuing choices that line up with their group creation, equilibrium, and generally vision. The science between group proprietors, the board, and the training staff is crucial during the sale, where parted second choices can shape the direction of a group's season. Fruitful establishments show a cooperative energy in their way to deal with player acquisitions, utilizing group science to fabricate a balanced crew.

The effect of group science in T20 cricket is maybe generally articulated during association stages and knockout matches. Groups that have developed a positive and firm group culture frequently track down an additional stuff during essential experiences. The science between players turns into a wellspring of solidarity during must-dominate matches, high-pressure pursues, or unequivocal minutes in a competition. Fruitful T20 groups exhibit a strength and solidarity that rise above individual exhibitions.

The significance of group science in T20 cricket is reflected in the job of group building exercises and holding meetings. Establishments coordinate off-field occasions, group meals, and exercises that advance kinship and common comprehension among players. These drives add to the human part of group science, cultivating fellowships, and making a feeling of fraternity inside the crew. Groups that focus on group building exercises frequently find that the bonds fashioned off the field convert into better comprehension and coordination on the field.

6.2 Building a balanced squad with varied skill sets

Building a reasonable crew with shifted ranges of abilities is an essential basic in T20 cricket, where the dynamic and speedy nature of the configuration requests a different arrangement of capacities to explore the difficulties presented by rivals and match circumstances. The development of a T20 crew includes a cautious mix of batting capability, bowling profundity, all-round capacities, handling ability, and key sharpness. A fair crew adjusts to differing match conditions as well as boosts strategic choices, making a considerable power fit for dealing with the erratic idea of T20 cricket.

One of the essential contemplations in building a decent T20 crew is the piece of the batting setup. An effective T20 group regularly includes a blend of hazardous openers, flexible center request batsmen, and finishers with the capacity to gain by the end phases of an innings. The openers set the vibe, giving the group a speedy beginning, while the center request balances out the innings and the finishers execute in the demise overs. The consideration of players with changed batting styles and jobs adds profundity and versatility to the crew, permitting the group to counter assorted bowling assaults and match situations.

The significance of all-rounders in building a reasonable T20 crew couldn't possibly be more significant. All-rounders contribute with both bat and ball, giving groups adaptability, profundity, and key choices. A quality all-rounder fortifies the batting and bowling offices as well as upgrades the group's flexibility to various match circumstances. The capacity to flawlessly progress between jobs — contributing as a finisher, playing as a bleeding edge bowler, or giving forward leaps the ball — makes all-rounders important resources in T20 cricket.

Bowling profundity is a foundation of an even T20 crew. Fruitful groups include a blend of speed and twist bowlers, each offering their interesting varieties and qualities of real value. The incorporation of experienced pacers fit for conveying searing spells, supplemented by talented spinners who can take advantage of turning tracks or trick batsmen with varieties, makes a balanced bowling assault. The essential utilization of bowlers who can execute in powerplays, contain in the center overs, and convey under tension in death overs is fundamental for a group's prosperity.

Handling ability is a non-debatable viewpoint in the development of a decent T20 crew. In an organization where each run and each wicket matters, spry and caution defenders can make game-evolving commitments. A solid handling unit saves runs as well as makes extra tension on the resistance. Groups that focus on handling greatness in their crew determinations frequently find that tight handling and gymnastic gets can swing the energy of a match in support of themselves.

Vital keenness is a range of abilities that reaches out past individual exhibitions and saturates the group's dynamic interaction. A fair T20 crew incorporates players who can peruse match circumstances, pursue informed choices under tension, and adjust their strategies in view of the resistance and the circumstances. The presence of experienced pioneers, players with a profound comprehension of the organization, and those with a history of effective captaincy improves the group's essential keenness.

With regards to T20 associations like the Indian Chief Association (IPL), the sale turns into a crucial stage for building a fair crew. Establishments should explore spending plan limitations, key offering wars, and the capriciousness of player valuations to collect a crew that lines up with their vision. The sale cycle includes a fragile harmony between getting marquee players, recognizing an incentive for-cash picks, and decisively filling explicit expertise holes inside the crew.

The marquee players, frequently global stars with a demonstrated history in T20 cricket, bring star power, insight, and game abilities to dominate to the crew. Establishments focus on these players for their singular splendor as well as for the effect they can have in group elements and execution. The essential procurement of marquee players includes cautious thought of their similarity with the group's playing style, initiative characteristics, and flexibility to various match conditions.

An incentive for-cash picks are similarly vital in building a fair T20 crew. Establishments should recognize underestimated players who bring particular abilities, undiscovered capacity, or explicit game dominating characteristics. The capacity to recognize unlikely treasures in the bartering, secure them at ideal costs, and influence their abilities decisively adds profundity and variety to the crew. Effective establishments frequently exhibit canny exploring, information investigation, and a profound comprehension of player elements to make keen picks during the closeout.

The crew building process in T20 cricket likewise includes making a harmony among experience and youth. While experienced players bring an abundance of information, poise under tension, and the capacity to coach more youthful gifts, arising players infuse energy, excitement, and an intrepid way to deal with the crew. The essential joining of youth and experience guarantees a unique group culture that values coherence while embracing the developing scene of T20 cricket.

Group balance reaches out to the variety of ranges of abilities inside the crew. The incorporation of players with particular abilities — like power-hitters, shrewd spinners, or demise overs trained professionals — adds layers to the group's strategic choices. The crew should be prepared to deal with an assortment of match situations, from pursuing enormous sums to guarding unobtrusive scores, and the presence of players with changed ranges of abilities considers vital versatility.

The job of the training staff in building a reasonable T20 crew is instrumental. Mentors should survey the qualities and shortcomings of every player, devise techniques that advance their commitments, and establish a climate that cultivates individual and aggregate development. The care staff, including batting mentors, bowling trainers, and handling mentors, assume a pivotal part in improving the abilities of players and guaranteeing that the crew capabilities as a durable unit.

Player accessibility and wellness contemplations are indispensable to crew balance. In the unique scene of T20 cricket, where players partake in various associations and worldwide responsibilities, overseeing player jobs turns into an essential goal. A fair crew incorporates players who can keep up with top wellness all through the season, diminishing the gamble of wounds and guaranteeing that the group can handle its best XI in essential matches.

The idea of job definition is foremost in building a decent T20 crew. Players should have an unmistakable comprehension of their jobs inside the group — whether as a power-hitting opener, a center request stabilizer, a passing overs trained professional, or a cutting edge spinner. Job clearness permits players to zero in on their assets, contribute actually in unambiguous circumstances, and adjust their singular exhibitions to the group's general procedure.

The effect of building a reasonable crew is generally obvious during the association stages and knockout matches. Groups that have effectively gathered a crew with changed ranges of abilities exhibit versatility and flexibility in various match circumstances. Whether it's pursuing a difficult objective, setting a defendable aggregate, or planning against explicit resistance qualities, a decent crew guarantees that the group can move toward each game with a thoroughly examined plan.

The essential utilization of player revolutions, particularly in lengthy competitions like the IPL, adds to crew balance. Groups should oversee player jobs, give potential open doors to all crew individuals, and settle on informed choices in light of structure, wellness, and match conditions. The capacity to turn players consistently, without compromising the general group balance, adds profundity to the crew and guarantees that each player remains match-prepared.

6.3 Challenges of managing diverse player personalities

Overseeing different player characters is a diverse test that defies mentors, group the executives, and initiative in different games, and cricket is no exemption. In the dynamic and high-pressure climate of expert cricket, where individual exhibitions contribute fundamentally to group achievement, figuring out, embracing, and successfully overseeing different characters is urgent for encouraging group union, improving execution, and keeping a positive group culture.

One of the essential difficulties in overseeing different player characters is the sheer assortment of foundations, societies, and dispositions that players bring to a group. Cricket, being a worldwide game, frequently sees players from various nations, identities, and cricketing frameworks uniting. The conflict of different foundations can prompt correspondence obstructions, misinterpretations, and difficulties in building a durable group culture. Fruitful administration requires an enthusiasm for social subtleties, an accentuation on inclusivity, and a proactive way to deal with encouraging comprehension among players.

Administration styles likewise assume a vital part in the administration of different player characters. Every player might answer contrastingly to different initiative methodologies, going from legitimate to participative. Commanders and training staff should tailor their initiative styles to oblige the inclinations and awarenesses of individual players. A one-size-fits-all approach is probably not going to be successful, and adaptability in administration techniques is fundamental for building trust and compatibility with different characters.

The conflict of self images is a typical test in overseeing high-profile players with solid characters. In a game like cricket, where individual exhibitions are firmly examined, players frequently convey a deep satisfaction and self-esteem. Adjusting the goals and self images of headliners while encouraging an aggregate group ethos requires insightful initiative. It includes establishing a climate where individual achievements are commended yet not to the detriment of the group's targets.

Correspondence breakdowns are one more critical obstacle in overseeing different player characters. Viable correspondence isn't just about passing on data yet in addition about understanding the remarkable correspondence styles of every player. A few players might favor immediate and confident correspondence, while others might answer better to a more strong and cooperative methodology. Exploring these distinctions requires open channels of correspondence, undivided attention, and a guarantee to settling clashes valuably.

Overseeing player assumptions is a fragile part of managing different characters. Players get groups together with differed assumptions about their jobs, playing time, and open doors. Adjusting these assumptions, particularly when there are restricted spots in the playing XI, requests straightforward correspondence and proactive player the board. Mentors and group the board should set practical assumptions, give lucidity on jobs, and take part in continuous exchange to oversee player goals.

The job of senior players in tutoring and coordinating more youthful gifts adds one more layer of intricacy to overseeing different player characters. While experienced players carry administration and security to the group, their associations with more youthful players can affect group elements. The test lies in guaranteeing a sound mentorship dynamic, where senior players guide and backing without establishing a climate of progressive system or disruptiveness.

Player burnout is a critical worry in cricket, given the feverish timetables, consistent travel, and the psychological cost of high-stakes rivalries. Overseeing different player characters includes perceiving the indications of burnout, understanding the novel stressors looked by every player, and carrying out procedures for mental prosperity. This requires a proactive way to deal with responsibility the executives, rest and recuperation, and giving players the fundamental emotional wellness support.

One more test in overseeing assorted player characters is taking care of players with various persuasive triggers. While certain players blossom with outside acknowledgment and prizes, others might be roused by interior factors like individual improvement or group achievement. Mentors and group the executives should tailor their persuasive methodologies to line up with the singular inclinations of players, guaranteeing that every individual from the group feels roused and put resources into the aggregate objectives.

The effect of off-field issues in group elements is a test that can't be disregarded. Players might be managing individual difficulties, family issues, or outer tensions that can influence their on-field execution and communications with partners. Group the board should be compassionate, strong, and proactive in addressing these off-field difficulties to guarantee that they don't subvert group solidarity or individual prosperity.

Group building exercises and holding meetings become fundamental apparatuses for overseeing assorted player characters. Setting out open doors for players to associate, share encounters, and construct special interactions cultivates fellowship and common comprehension. Fruitful groups frequently focus on group building drives that go past cricket, permitting players to interface on a human level and value the variety inside the crew.

In a game where feelings run high, overseeing player clashes is a continuous test. Contrasting sentiments, cutthroat pressures, and individual desires can prompt struggles inside the group. Mentors and group the executives should go about as middle people, working with open and helpful discourse to determine clashes. A culture that urges players to communicate their interests, gives instruments to compromise, and stresses aggregate objectives over individual complaints is urgent for keeping up with group concordance.

The test of overseeing different player characters is additionally emphasizd during competitions like the Indian Head Association (IPL), where players from different cricketing societies meet up to address an establishment. The time imperatives, extraordinary rivalry, and the requirement for sure fire attachment request proactive measures in group the executives. Effective IPL establishments focus on early group holding, make a comprehensive group culture, and influence the qualities of different characters to fabricate an imposing crew.

The presentation of player barters in T20 associations like the IPL adds an extra layer of intricacy to overseeing different player characters. Establishments should explore the sale room in a calculated way, pursuing choices that line up with group sythesis, equilibrium, and in general vision. The elements of sell-offs, with contending offers and the component of shock, can influence player elements inside a crew. Viable administration includes guaranteeing that players feel esteemed and upheld, no matter what the conditions of their procurement.

Overseeing different player characters is a continuous interaction that requires flexibility and a promise to persistent improvement. The capacity of instructing staff and group the board to develop their techniques in light of criticism, changing group elements, and the advancing necessities of individual players is significant. This requires a development outlook, an eagerness to learn, and a receptiveness to imaginative methodologies in player the board.

Chapter 7

The Unpredictable Twists

The universe of cricket, frequently hailed as a round of vulnerabilities, is no more bizarre to the eccentric exciting bends in the road that shape the story of matches and competitions. From dazzling rebounds to unexpected breakdowns, the game's intrinsic dynamism adds a component of tension and fervor that enraptures fans all over the planet. These eccentric turns characterize the pith of cricket as well as add to the game's getting through appeal.

One of the most arresting parts of cricket's flightiness lies in the fluctuating fortunes of groups during a match, particularly in designs like Test cricket and One Day Internationals (ODIs). A group that appears to be near the very edge of triumph can end up wrestling with an unexpected breakdown, while a longshot group can surprise everyone and organize a striking circle back. This rhythmic movement, frequently alluded to as the "energy shift," is a demonstration of the game's ability to shock and keep fans as eager and anxious as can be.

The component of capriciousness is maybe most articulated with regards to batting breakdowns — a peculiarity that can reverse the situation of a match in a matter of seconds.

Whether it's a series of wickets falling one after another or a breakdown set off by outstanding bowling exhibitions, the delicacy of a group's batting request highlights the fine edges among progress and disappointment in cricket. The unconventionality of batting breakdowns adds show and power to the game, as groups wrestle with the test of recuperating from tricky circumstances.

Bowling spells that make heads spin and grandstand individual splendor are one more wellspring of cricket's unusual turns. A bowler, apparently unexceptional in prior phases of a match, can out of nowhere release a staggering spell that destroys the resistance's batting setup. The unusualness of champion bowling exhibitions adds a component of interest to the game, as bowlers become the engineers of urgent minutes that shape the result of matches.

Weather patterns, a variable past the control of players, further add to cricket's eccentric nature. Downpour interferences, particularly in restricted overs designs, can change match elements, impact target estimations, and power groups to change their methodologies on the fly. The vulnerability presented by climate related interferences adds a layer of intricacy to cricket, with groups and fans the same left to consider the "what-uncertainties" notwithstanding nature's impulses.

Cricket's flightiness isn't restricted to individual matches however stretches out to whole competitions and series. Longshot groups, discounted before the beginning of a contest, can blow some minds and arise as surprisingly strong contenders, causing significant bombshells and reshaping the competition's story. The eccentric directions of groups in lengthy structure series or multi-group competitions add to the game's allure, as fans revel in the vulnerability of results and the potential for dark horse wins.

The idea of tie coordinates and attracted results Test cricket typifies the unusual idea of the game. A match that appears to be set out toward a specific outcome can observer an emotional new development, prompting an intriguing halt where neither one of the groups arises successful. Tie matches and draws highlight the strength of groups, the meaning of individual exhibitions, and the limit of cricket to deliver results that overcome ordinary presumption.

The coming of T20 cricket, with its speedy and high-scoring nature, has acquainted another aspect with cricket's eccentricism. The organization's quickness, combined with the interest for forceful play, frequently prompts fast changes in energy, touchy batting showcases, and nail-gnawing wraps up. The eccentricism of T20 cricket is exemplified by the potential for last-over thrill rides, where a solitary conveyance can decide the destiny of the match.

Cricket's eccentric turns are not restricted to on-handle activity; they reach out to the off-field elements of the game also.

Determination shocks, key choices by group the executives, and unforeseen retirements add a component of unusualness to the by and large cricketing scene. The cricketing society, including players, fans, and intellectuals, should continually adjust to the unexpected advancements that shape the game's account.

The Indian Head Association (IPL), a grandstand of T20 cricket, is a favorable place for erratic turns. The sale cycle, where establishments seek player marks, frequently brings about startling group sytheses and player mixes. Marquee players, expected to be the key parts of a group's mission, can confront unforeseen downturns in structure, while moderately obscure players can arise as breakout stars. The ease of group elements and player exhibitions in the IPL embodies the unusual pith of T20 cricket.

The job of individual splendor in molding cricket's unusual story couldn't possibly be more significant. Batsmen who release rankling hundreds of years from apparently inconceivable circumstances, bowlers who invoke otherworldly spells, and defenders who pull off stunning gets — all add to the irregular snapshots of splendor that reclassify the course of a match. These singular heroics become the impetuses for unusual turns that hoist the energy levels of the game.

The complexities of cricket's scoring framework add one more layer to its eccentricism. The presentation of Choice Survey Framework (DRS) innovation, pointed toward decreasing umpiring blunders, has prompted emotional snapshots of vulnerability and expectation. The eccentricism of DRS results, with surveys frequently depending on fine edges and innovation helped choices changing match situations, adds another aspect to the show of cricket.

Eccentric results likewise reach out to player structure and exhibitions over-stretched periods. A player who enters a series with a productive run of structure might experience a startling rut, while an out-of-structure player can organize a re-bound with a series-characterizing execution. The capacity of players to explore the pinnacles and box of structure, and the unconventionality of individual directions, add to the game's getting through stories.

The brain science of the game, impacted by pressure circumstances, the heaviness of assumptions, and the psychological strength of players, further improves cricket's eccentric turns. The elements of a high-pressure pursue, where an apparently reachable objective changes into a nerve-wracking pursuit, represent the mental rollercoaster that players and fans insight. The flightiness of player reactions to pressure circumstances adds a component of human show to the game.

Cricket's flightiness isn't restricted to global or proficient cricket; it penetrates the texture of the game at all levels. From grassroots cricket to nearby associations, surprising exhibitions, close gets done, and capricious results are woven into the game's DNA. The appeal of cricket lies in its capacity to shock and enthrall, making each match, no matter what the level, a material for flighty turns.

7.1 Unexpected turn of events in the auction

The bartering room, with its demeanor of expectation, key moving, and flighty offering wars, fills in as the heartbeat of T20 cricket associations like the Indian Chief Association (IPL). It is in this unique field that the surprising development frequently becomes the dominant focal point, reshaping the fortunes of establishments, changing group pieces, and leaving fans and specialists the same in stunningness. The exciting bends in the road in the closeout are not just a demonstration of the unstable idea of player valuations yet in addition an impression of the perplexing dance of methodology and unusualness.

One of the most spellbinding parts of the closeout is the rise of startling offering battles for marquee players. While specific players enter the sale with elevated requirements, establishments some of the time shock everybody by forcefully chasing after a specific player, driving the offering past expected levels. The startling heightening of offers can be credited to various elements, including a player's new heavenly exhibitions, explicit group prerequisites, or a serious rivalry among establishments anxious to get a unique advantage.

The surprising development in the sale is in many cases filled by the essential moves of establishments chasing marquee players. Groups might take on capricious offering procedures, for example, intentionally swelling the cost for an opponent establishment or decisively pulling out from offering at a basic point to control the last worth of a player. The capriciousness of these essential moves adds a component of tension to the sale, as establishments take part in a high-stakes chess game to outsmart their rivals.

The job of uncapped players in the closeout presents an extra layer of flightiness. While laid out global stars order consideration and powerful sticker prices, uncapped players can turn into the unexpected bundles of the bartering. Establishments enthusiastic about uncovering unlikely treasures frequently participate in vivacious offering battles for gifted at this point moderately obscure players, prompting startling results and changing the elements of group organizations.

Wounds and last-minute withdrawals of marquee players can set off unanticipated occasions in the bartering room. Establishments, carefully arranging their systems around specific central members, may wind up constrained to adjust on the fly when confronted with the unexpected inaccessibility of a headliner.

This surprising new development can prompt a reshuffling of needs, wild reexaminations of group needs, and a competition to get elective choices before the sale finishes up.

The eccentricism of the closeout is increased by the presence of establishment proprietors, each with their extraordinary styles, inclinations, and monetary ability. Proprietors, driven by an enthusiasm for the game and a longing for progress, can infuse surprising energy into the procedures. Striking and rash choices by establishment proprietors, whether chasing after marquee players or the essential arrangement of their spending plan, add to the eccentric story of the sale.

The rise of unforeseen surprisingly strong contenders among establishments adds one more layer of interest to the sale. While specific establishments are enduring top picks for their monetary may and vital keenness, the flighty idea of T20 cricket guarantees that longshot groups can disturb the laid out request. A less popular establishment might spring shocks by making key purchases, outmaneuvering their rivals, and gathering a cutthroat crew despite everything.

Player elements, including last-minute accessibility changes, wellness concerns, or late passages into the bartering pool, can present surprising turns. Players who were not at first on the radar may out of nowhere become sought-after items, prompting fast changes in offering elements. Establishments, equipped with constant data, should adjust quickly to these unforeseen improvements to gain by arising open doors or relieve chances.

The idea of Right to Match (RTM) cards in the closeout framework presents an extra layer of flightiness. Establishments can send RTM cards to hold explicit players from their past crews, tossing a vital curve into the offering system. The unforeseen utilization of RTM cards for specific players can adjust the coloring of the bartering, leaving establishments and fans the same estimating on the maintenance systems utilized by each group.

The impact of player specialists and their exchanges with establishments adds a fascinating aspect to the closeout's flightiness. In the background conversations, last-minute exchanges, and the sensitive dance of player portrayal can impact offering elements and change a player's fairly estimated worth. The unforeseen turns in player-specialist talks frequently become known during the closeout, astounding the two onlookers and establishments with the results.

The bartering's configuration, with its quick fire offering adjusts and the tension of pursuing split-subsequent options, amplifies the effect of unforeseen developments. Establishments should explore the bartering's excited speed, go with vital choices progressively, and adjust to quickly evolving situations. The startling turns in offering elements can prompt extemporaneous recalibrations of group procedures, as establishments endeavor to construct a cutthroat crew inside the imperatives of their financial plans.

The idea of 'shock picks' in the bartering adds a component of capriciousness to group arrangements. Establishments might spring shocks by choosing players who were not generally expected to draw in huge offers. These unexpected picks can be arising abilities, players with remarkable ranges of abilities, or people who have performed astoundingly well in homegrown or worldwide T20 associations. The startling incorporation of such players changes up group programs.

The offering battles for explicit ranges of abilities or player jobs can bring about startling results. Establishments might end up participated in extraordinary fights for players who have specific abilities pivotal for their group's requirements. Whether it's a power-hitting batsman, a passing overs expert bowler, or a shrewd spinner, the unforeseen expansion of offers for players with explicit qualities can reshape group sytheses and modify the normal equilibrium of crews.

The elements of the closeout can be affected by outside factors, like media stories, public opinion, or the apparent worth of specific players. Establishments might wind up influenced by outside assumptions, prompting surprising choices in player acquisitions. Media buzz encompassing explicit players, fan responses, and the more extensive cricketing talk can bring a component of flightiness into the dynamic cycles of establishments.

Startling new development can likewise appear as essential movements by establishments during the closeout. A group at first zeroing in on building an imposing batting setup may unexpectedly change gears to focus on supporting its bowling assault, in light of the unfurling elements of the bartering. These essential turns can be set off by the surprising accessibility of specific players, the development of serious offering for explicit jobs, or the advancing necessities of the group.

The post-sell off examination and responses from specialists and fans frequently feature the surprising accounts that unfurled during the offering system. Astounding picks, unexpected valuations, and the essential masterstrokes or errors of establishments become arguments, adding an additional layer of show and conversation to the repercussions of the sale. The surprising disclosures and bits of knowledge gathered from present sale examinations contribute on the continuous interest and hypothesis encompassing T20 associations.

7.2 Last-minute bidding strategies and surprises

The last minutes of a player closeout in T20 cricket associations like the Indian Chief Association (IPL) are similar to the peak of an emotional thrill ride. Establishments, outfitted with restricted time and financial plans, decisively disclose their somewhat late offering methodologies, expecting to get the last bits of their ideal crew. This period of the bartering is a landmark of mind, nerve, and instinct, where shocks unfurl, and the destiny of players remains in a critical state.

One of the most widely recognized somewhat late offering procedures is the purposeful defer in offering for marquee players. Establishments might decide to await their chance, allowing different groups to debilitate their financial plans right off the bat in the closeout, just to plunge in later for vital offers on players they esteem exceptionally. This strategic persistence can prompt unforeseen turns, with establishments decisively keeping their offers until the last snapshots of the sale.

The somewhat late offering free for all frequently strengthens for players who certainly stand out prior in the bartering. Establishments, conscious of their leftover financial plan and group piece needs, may unexpectedly go into energetic offering battles for players who offer explicit ranges of abilities or fill essential jobs. These late-breaking offering wars infuse a flood of energy into the bartering room, as establishments rider to get misjudged gifts.

Late-stage shocks in offering can likewise be coordinated by establishments hoping to make an essential effect on their rivals. An unexpected forceful bid for a player, particularly one who was not on the radar of different establishments, can disturb the financial plan estimations and masterful plans of opponent groups. This component of shock is a determined move to disrupt rivals and position an establishment as a smart player in the sale elements.

The Option to Match (RTM) cards, an essential instrument permitting establishments to hold explicit players from their past crews, frequently become possibly the most important factor as a somewhat late offering technique. Establishments may decisively convey their RTM cards for central participants in the last snapshots of the bartering, amazing different groups and getting the administrations of players who have demonstrated their value in past seasons. The essential utilization of RTM cards adds a layer of unconventionality to the end phases of the closeout.

Late-stage offering procedures are not restricted to players but rather additionally reach out to explicit jobs or ranges of abilities that establishments try to support. An establishment may, in the last minutes, focus on a power-hitting batsman, a passing overs expert bowler, or a carefully prepared all-rounder to finish its crew. This engaged way to deal with late-stage offering mirrors the nuanced group building procedures that establishments utilize to address basic holes in their line-ups.

The idea of key financial plan designation turns out to be especially essential somewhat recently of the closeout. Establishments, with a limited spending plan available to them, should reasonably designate their leftover assets to get the players they focus on. The essential appropriation of assets in the last stages includes measuring the market worth of players, surveying the necessities of the crew, and going with on-the-fly choices to expand the group's general strength.

Somewhat late astonishments additionally exude from the perplexing dance of establishments dealing with their abroad and homegrown player amounts. Groups, particularly in associations with limitations on the quantity of abroad players in the playing XI, should explore the sensitive equilibrium of getting global stars while guaranteeing a balanced crew with a blend of homegrown gifts. The last minutes of the closeout frequently witness startling choices and shock picks as establishments calibrate their abroad and homegrown player mixes.

The job of group proprietors and leaders turns out to be especially articulated somewhat recently of the sale. Proprietors, driven by a blend of key vision and close to home speculation, may declare their impact with latest possible moment mandates or inclinations. Their contribution can prompt unforeseen turns, like an unexpected push for a marquee player, an improvised change in group system, or a strong key move that overcomes traditional presumption.

Late-stage offering systems are not just impacted by the longing to get explicit players yet in addition by the need to keep up with adaptability and flexibility in group sytheses. Establishments may decisively keep down a piece of their spending plan for the last minutes, permitting them to gain by unanticipated open doors, address surprising holes, or take strategic actions because of the developing elements of the sale.

The elements of somewhat late offering additionally witness the development of overlooked yet truly great individuals — players who, until the last stages, stayed inconspicuous however out of nowhere turned into the point of convergence of serious offering wars. These slowpokes, frequently uncapped or less proclaimed, feature their abilities at the center of the last minutes, prompting vivacious challenges among establishments anxious to get their administrations. The eccentricism of these late-stage disclosures adds a component of energy to the sale.

The effect of wounds or wellness concerns can set off somewhat late changes in offering methodologies. Establishments, confronted with surprising improvements in regards to the accessibility of specific players, should quickly recalibrate their arrangements. This might include diverting offers towards elective players, returning to their group piece systems, or settling on speedy choices to alleviate the effect of unexpected difficulties.

The sale room's climate during the last minutes is accused of strain, fervor, and a need to get moving. Establishments, with a restricted window of time staying, should pursue split-subsequent options that can shape the predetermination of their crews for the impending season. The discernible energy in the last minutes, combined with the unconventionality of late-stage offering, makes an exhilarating exhibition for fans and partners the same.

Late-stage offering isn't exclusively determined by player valuations yet additionally by the essential evaluation of a player's similarity with the group's playing style, crew prerequisites, and generally vision.

Establishments, furnished with point by point exploring reports and vital experiences, influence their insight to settle on educated choices in the end organizes regarding the bartering. The interaction of information examination, cricketing keenness, and key premonition turns out to be especially obvious as establishments explore the intricacies of late-stage offering.

The unconventionality of somewhat late offering procedures is uplifted by the powerful idea of the bartering design itself. The fast progression of offers, counter-offers, and the ticking clock add a component of earnestness and power to the procedures. Groups should think and react quickly, respond quickly to arising valuable open doors or difficulties, and settle on sharp choices inside the limitations of time and financial plan.

Post-closeout examination frequently reveals insight into the essential subtleties and shocks that unfurled somewhat recently of the offering system. Eyewitnesses and savants analyze the late-stage choices, unforeseen picks, and the general effect of latest possible moment methodologies in the organization of groups. The post-closeout account reflects the determined moves of establishments as well as the unexpected turns that additional show to the last minutes.

7.3 Impact of unforeseen circumstances on team plans

The universe of cricket, with its dynamic and erratic nature, frequently tosses un-anticipated conditions at groups, testing their arrangements and versatility. From unexpected wounds to central members to startling climate disturbances, the effect of these unanticipated occasions can resonate all through a competition, series, or individual matches, compelling groups to adjust on the fly and test the profundity of their essential preparation.

Quite possibly of the most effective and normal unexpected situation in cricket is the event of wounds to central members. Whether it's a star batsman, a forefront bowler, or an essential all-rounder, wounds can fundamentally upset a group's arrangements and modify the equilibrium of the crew. The unexpected shortfall of a central member can drive groups to reexamine their techniques, reconsider their batting or bowling line-ups, and change their general strategy to adapt to the misfortune.

Wounds influence the on-field elements as well as posture difficulties for group the board concerning player turns and responsibility the executives. The unforeseen sidelining of a player might require changes in the group's pivot strategy, influencing the arranged rest and recuperation periods for other crew individuals. Group the board should explore these difficulties while guaranteeing that the general wellness and execution levels of the crew are kept up with.

Climate related disturbances address one more arrangement of unexpected conditions that can essentially impact group plans in cricket.

Downpour deferrals, interferences, or even total wastes of time can compel groups to reevaluate their systems, particularly in restricted overs designs where the designation of overs is urgent. Groups might have to change their batting orders, reexamine target computations, or pursue speedy choices on bowling methodologies in light of the amended playing conditions.

The effect of climate related interruptions reaches out past the prompt match and can have gradually expanding influences on the general timetable of a series or competition. Rescheduled matches, packed installations, or consecutive games because of downpour initiated changes can test a group's physical and mental perseverance. Crews might wind up wrestling with the test of overseeing player weariness, keeping up with maximized operation levels, and adjusting to a changed cadence of play.

The development of unexpected conditions can likewise appear as off-field interruptions or contentions that influence group elements. Issues, for example, contract debates, disciplinary issues, or unforeseen retirements can make disturbances inside the crew, requiring group the executives to explore sensitive relational elements and keep a durable group culture. These off-field difficulties can affect player spirit, center, and the general group climate.

The choice issues emerging from unanticipated conditions further add intricacy to group plans. Wounds or startling advancements might prompt somewhat late changes in the playing XI, driving groups to reevaluate their mixes and procedures. The determination of substitution players, particularly in high-stakes competitions, requires canny decision-production to guarantee that the picked players flawlessly coordinate into the group dynamic and contribute successfully.

The capriciousness of player accessibility, affected by variables like wellness, structure, or outside responsibilities, acquaints one more layer of intricacy with group arranging. Players taking part in different associations, worldwide visits, or overseeing individual responsibilities might experience unanticipated planning clashes that influence their accessibility for certain matches or periods of a competition. Groups should explore these provokes and pursue key choices to improve the accessibility of central members.

The effect of unanticipated conditions is especially articulated in T20 associations like the Indian Head Association (IPL), where establishments assemble their crews through sell-offs and player drafts. Wounds or withdrawals of marquee players previously or during the competition can compel groups into a scramble to track down reasonable substitutions. The elements of player barters, with its spending plan requirements and cutthroat offering, add an additional layer of intricacy to the most common way of obtaining substitution players.

The abrupt accessibility of worldwide players because of changes in their public group plans or surprising retirements can likewise impact group plans.

Establishments should survey the possible effect of such players in group elements, change their procedures likewise, and pursue vital choices on whether to offer for or hold these players. The smoothness of player accessibility brings a component of unconventionality into group creation.

The effect of unexpected conditions in group plans isn't restricted to in-prepare changes yet additionally reaches out to the pre-competition planning stage. Groups put huge time and assets in planning, rehearsing, and calibrating their arrangements in front of a competition. In any case, surprising occasions, for example, a central participant being precluded because of injury or an adjustment of the training staff, can require quick recalibrations in the group's methodology.

The complexities of overseeing unexpected conditions expect groups to develop flexibility and versatility as fundamental credits. The capacity to answer successfully to unforeseen difficulties, go with fast choices under tension, and keep a positive group culture notwithstanding difficulty becomes significant. Fruitful groups influence unanticipated conditions as any open doors for development, learning, and reinforcing their general group elements.

The effect of unexpected conditions in group plans isn't restricted to strategic or key contemplations; it additionally reaches out to the psychological part of the game. Players and groups should explore the mental difficulties that emerge from surprising misfortunes, whether it's the passing of a central member, a line of horrible outcomes, or off-field interruptions. Mental mettle, administration versatility, and an aggregate obligation to beating difficulties assume crucial parts in deciding a group's reaction to unexpected conditions.

With regards to worldwide cricket, the difficulties presented by movement limitations, bio-bubbles, and the worldwide wellbeing scene during the Coronavirus pandemic have added another aspect to unanticipated conditions. Groups should battle with the vulnerabilities of visiting, quarantine prerequisites, and the expected effect of positive cases on crew accessibility. The requirement for careful preparation, severe wellbeing conventions, and possibility measures has become essential to the advanced cricketing scene.

The effect of unexpected conditions isn't exclusively a test; it likewise presents a chance for groups to exhibit their versatility and capacity to flourish under tension. Snapshots of misfortune can become characterizing sections in a group's excursion, uncovering the personality of players, the viability of group the board, and the strength of the group's general ethos. Fruitful groups frequently arise more grounded and more durable from unexpected difficulties.

Chapter 8

From Auction Table to Playing Field

The excursion from the closeout table to the battleground in T20 cricket associations like the Indian Head Association (IPL) is an entrancing investigation of group building methodologies, player elements, and the unfurling show of a profoundly serious and dynamic brandishing scene. As establishments carefully gather their crews through sell-offs, drafts, and vital direction, the progress from the bartering table to the battleground addresses the perfection of long periods of arranging, expectation, and high-stakes speculations.

The sale table, the operational hub of T20 cricket associations, is where establishments participate in wild fights to get the administrations of players who line up with their essential vision. The interaction starts with the exploring and pre-sell off investigation, where groups recognize key areas of progress, evaluate crew necessities, and decide the profiles of players that fit their arrangements. This stage lays the foundation for the bartering technique, affecting offering targets, spending plan allotments, and generally crew structure.

The marquee players, frequently the key parts of a group's system, draw at the center of attention at the closeout table. Establishments, furnished with their spending plans and key needs, take part in serious offering battles for these high-profile players. The result of these fights shapes the center of a group as well as establishes the vibe until the end of the closeout. The fruitful securing of marquee players is a basic achievement, flagging a group's purpose and laying out the establishment for its mission on the battleground.

As the closeout advances, establishments explore the intricacies of player valuations, financial plan requirements, and vital needs. The quest for a fair crew, with a blend of experienced campaigners and arising gifts, becomes fundamental. Groups decisively bid for players who bring different ranges of abilities, tending to explicit jobs, for example, power-hitting, passing bowling, or twist varieties. The bartering table turns into a venue of key navigation, with establishments cautiously adjusting their speculations to make a balanced group.

The idea of uncapped players adds a component of eccentricism to the sale, as establishments strive for generally obscure gifts who can possibly become breakout stars. The effective recognizable proof and procurement of uncapped players can essentially influence a group's fortunes on the battleground, infusing energetic richness, new viewpoints, and surprising exhibitions. The sale table turns into a phase for uncovering unexpected, yet invaluable treasures and reshaping the story of a group's excursion.

The closeout's elements are additionally impacted by the essential utilization of apparatuses, for example, Right to Match (RTM) cards. Establishments convey RTM cards to hold players from their past crews, presenting a component of congruity and commonality. The decision-production around RTM cards requires a fragile harmony between holding center players and decisively offering for new increments. The interaction of RTM cards shapes the direction of groups, permitting them to mix coherence with imbuement of new ability.

From the sale table, groups progress to the post-closeout stage, where they participate in extra player acquisitions through exchanges, moves, and supplemental drafts. This stage fills in as a chance to adjust crew arrangements, address any holes distinguished during the sale, and further fortify the group in front of the playing season. The post-sell off moves mirror the continuous vital development of groups as they get ready for the difficulties on the field.

The change from the sale table to the battleground includes a change in center from key wanting to strategic execution. Mentors, support staff, and players set out on a concentrated arrangement stage, including instructional courses, practice matches, and vital meetings. The test lies in deciphering the essential plan made at the bartering table into a firm and high-performing unit on the battleground.

Player combination turns into a critical part of the progress from the closeout table to the battleground. Groups should cultivate a feeling of fellowship, understanding, and divided objectives between players from different foundations and playing styles. The training staff assumes a crucial part in adjusting individual yearnings to group goals, making a culture of joint effort, and imparting an aggregate feeling of direction. The fruitful combination of players into the group texture is fundamental for on-field achievement.

Group elements, frequently molded by the authority style of skippers and mentors, go through ceaseless refinement as the playing season draws near. Commanders should find some kind of harmony between giving key course and encouraging a climate where players feel enabled to communicate their innovativeness and senses on the field. The change to the battleground requires a consistent arrangement of initiative vision, player jobs, and strategic adaptability.

The battleground, with its energizing environment, intense groups, and the strain of execution, is a definitive field where groups exhibit the products of their bartering table methodologies. The initial match denotes the start of the excursion, and groups should quickly adjust to the cadence and force of serious T20 cricket. The battleground turns into a material where systems are tried, players display their abilities, and the elements of the crew are put to a definitive test.

The job of marquee players, the highlights of groups' closeout methodologies, is amplified on the battleground. These players are supposed to show others how its done, shoulder the obligation of game dominating exhibitions, and give the driving force to their groups. The change from the closeout table to the battleground sees marquee players venturing into the spotlight, confronting the assumptions and examination that accompany their high-profile status.

The effect of uncapped players, the unlikely treasures found at the closeout table, becomes apparent on the battleground. Uncapped players frequently bring a component of unconventionality, courage, and crude ability to the group. Their exhibitions can act as impetuses for progress, infusing energy into the crew and amazing rivals with their abilities. The battleground turns into a phase for uncapped players to report their appearance and cut a specialty for themselves.

The adequacy of group procedures made at the closeout table is reflected in the execution of plans on the battleground. Bowling assaults should convey as per the outline — whether it includes smothering resistance batsmen in the powerplay, sending particular demise bowlers, or presenting turn varieties decisively. Batting line-ups should adjust to match circumstances, offset animosity with strength, and benefit from key open doors.

The battleground additionally witnesses the development of startling legends — players who, in spite of not being the marquee names, assume urgent parts in their group's prosperity.

Whether it's a lower-request batsman conveying in a high-pressure pursue, an overlooked spinner picking pivotal wickets, or a defender taking stunning gets, these startling legends add to the story of the time. The battleground turns into a phase for unrecognized gifts to sparkle.

Wounds, one of the unanticipated conditions that groups plan for at the sale table, can affect the battleground elements. The profundity of a crew, the viability of reinforcement players, and the flexibility of group procedures are tried when central participants are sidelined because of wounds. The battleground turns into a pot where groups should show flexibility, mix assets, and explore difficulties presented by the unforeseen.

Climate related disturbances, one more component considered during vital preparation, can impact the battleground experience. Groups should acclimate to modified match conditions, shortened games, or even the chance of various matches one after another because of downpour prompted changes. The battleground turns into a material where flexibility and speedy dynamic because of unanticipated conditions are pivotal for progress.

The effect of the progress from the closeout table to the battleground is additionally apparent in the captaincy and vital decision-production during matches. Skippers must capably peruse the game, make constant strategic changes, and display initiative under tension. The battleground turns into a unique chessboard where skippers decisively convey their assets, evaluate match circumstances, and settle on striking choices that can shape the result.

The progress is additionally set apart by the advancement of group techniques all through the playing season. As groups progress through the competition or series, they accumulate experiences into their assets, shortcomings, and the elements of their adversaries. The battleground turns into a lab for key trial and error, refinement of strategies, and the ceaseless development of blueprints in view of continuous criticism.

The progress of establishments in T20 cricket associations is eventually estimated by their presentation on the battleground — the amassing of wins, the quest for season finisher billets, and the journey for title magnificence. The excursion from the closeout table to the battleground is a story bend that incorporates vital preparation, group building elements, and the unfurling show of on-field contest. It is an excursion where establishments explore the complexities of player acquisitions, adjust to unanticipated difficulties, and take a stab at on-field greatness in quest for T20 cricket's definitive award.

8.1 Transitioning from auction strategies to on-field tactics

The progress from closeout procedures to on-handle strategies in T20 cricket associations like the Indian Chief Association (IPL) addresses an essential stage in a group's excursion.

It denotes the development from vital preparation and player acquisitions to the powerful domain of match situations, key choices, and the execution of strategies on the field. This progress typifies the difficulties and complexities of making an interpretation of pre-season systems into on-field achievement, where skippers, mentors, and players should adjust, advance, and execute with accuracy.

At the core of this change lies the reconciliation of recently procured players into the group's current structure. While the sale methodologies center around recognizing players who supplement the group's vision, the on-field change requires a consistent mixing of different gifts, playing styles, and characters. The training staff assumes a basic part in cultivating a firm group culture, building fellowship, and guaranteeing that players get it and embrace their jobs inside the crew.

The marquee players, frequently the focal points of a group's closeout procedure, become the key parts of on-field strategies. The progress from the bartering table to the battleground sees these central members venturing into positions of authority, both with bat and ball, as they are supposed to establish the vibe for the group. Commanders should make on-field strategies that influence the qualities of marquee players, using their abilities decisively to boost influence in different match circumstances.

As groups progress to on-handle strategies, the subtleties of T20 cricket request an essential methodology that offsets hostility with logic. Batting procedures, for example, should be dynamic, adjusting to the match setting, the condition of the game, and the qualities and shortcomings of the resistance. The initial pair's methodology might contrast from that of center request batsmen, and the capacity to speed up or settle the innings turns into a critical feature of on-field strategies.

Bowling strategies, as well, go through essential development on the field. Groups should recognize key periods of the game — powerplays, center overs, and passing overs — and tailor their bowling techniques likewise. Commanders send their bowlers decisively, arriving at informed conclusions about when to present spinners, release quick bowlers, or use expert passing over bowlers. The on-field progress requests a strategic discernment that upgrades the assets accessible and takes advantage of resistance weaknesses.

Player jobs, a point of convergence during sell off procedures, show signs of life on the battleground. The assigned power-hitters should convey speedy runs, finishers must exhibit their ability in finishing off innings, and bowlers should execute their particular abilities with accuracy. The effective execution of on-field strategies depends on players understanding and embracing their jobs, permitting the group to work as a very much oiled unit where each individual adds to the aggregate achievement.

The eccentricism of T20 cricket presents a component of vital adaptability on the field. Chiefs should be lithe in their navigation, prepared to adjust to changing match circumstances, and make on-the-fly acclimations to their strategies. The on-field change expects commanders to peruse the game keenly, expect resistance moves, and pursue strategic choices that exploit potential open doors or moderate dangers as they emerge over the span of a match.

The effect of unanticipated conditions, a thought during sell off arranging, appears on the battleground. Wounds, abrupt changes in weather patterns, or unforeseen turns in the match situation can disturb biased strategies. The on-field change requests speedy reasoning and the capacity to recalibrate methodologies in light of these unexpected difficulties. Groups must exhibit strength, acclimate to the unforeseen, and remain created under tension.

From the bartering table to on-handle strategies, the idea of key profundity becomes significant. The seat strength, frequently gathered through insightful close-out arranging, becomes instrumental during the playing season. Groups should have elective methodologies and reinforcement choices set up, fit to be sent in light of match conditions, player structure, or strategic necessities. The in field change expects groups to use their crew profundity actually and guarantee that each player is ready to contribute when called upon.

The playing conditions, including pitch attributes, ground aspects, and winning climate, effect on-field strategies altogether. Groups should figure these factors while creating their methodologies, adjusting their approaches to suit the particular difficulties presented by every scene. The on-field change requires a comprehension of the novel elements of various playing surfaces and the capacity to likewise tailor strategies.

The job of information investigation, a device frequently utilized during sell off arranging, reaches out to on-handle strategies. Groups utilize constant information and execution examination to go with informed choices on the field. From surveying resistance player qualities and shortcomings to examining match examples and patterns, information driven experiences assume an essential part in molding on-field methodologies. The on-field progress highlights the marriage of cricketing sharpness with the force of information driven direction.

Group elements, a point of convergence during the progress, are continually developing on the battleground. The on-field climate is dynamic, with players encountering the rhythmic movement of feelings, the strain of match circumstances, and the requirement for compelling correspondence. Commanders and mentors should cultivate a positive group culture, impart certainty, and guarantee that the group stays joined in quest for its goals. The on-field change requests strategic insight as well as successful initiative and man-the executives abilities.

The idea of development comes to the front during the on-field change. Groups should explore different avenues regarding procedures, strategies, and player jobs to remain ahead in the powerful scene of T20 cricket.

From unusual field positions to imaginative bowling varieties, the capacity to shock rivals and adjust to arising patterns turns into a sign of effective on-field strategies. The on-field change supports a culture of development and versatility.

The power of the playing season, set apart by a pressed timetable and high-stakes matches, adds a layer of physical and mental weariness to the on-field change. Groups should oversee player jobs successfully, guaranteeing a harmony among execution and recuperation. The on-field change requests an exhaustive way to deal with wellness, molding, and mental versatility to endure the afflictions of a requesting season.

The progress from sell off methodologies to on-handle strategies likewise includes the usage of vital breaks. Groups can decisively stop the game, survey the match circumstance, and recalibrate their strategies during these spans. Chiefs, mentors, and players team up to adjust their arrangements, address arising difficulties, and set out to arrive at the rest of the match. The on-field change highlights the significance of key breaks as critical minutes for strategic recalibration.

The on-field progress is especially apparent during vital minutes like player excusals, key associations, or basic periods of the match. Chiefs should settle on vital choices, for example, presenting a particular bowler, setting forceful or guarded fields, or using survey choices prudently. The capacity to explore these essential minutes with balance and strategic sagacity turns into a characterizing factor in a group's on-field achievement.

The change from closeout techniques to on-handle strategies is epitomized chasing after season finisher compartments and title greatness. Groups should meet all requirements for the knockout stages as well as feature an elevated degree of strategic ability in high-pressure season finisher experiences. The on-field change requests an additional layer of vital complexity as groups compete for a definitive award, exploring the complexities of knockout cricket.

The zenith of the playing season addresses the full acknowledgment of the on-field progress. Groups ponder their excursion, the adequacy of their procedures, and the execution of on-field strategies. Achievement is estimated as far as wins and misfortunes as well as in the capacity to adjust, advance, and exhibit versatility despite challenges. The on-field progress is a story curve that traverses the whole season, from the sale table to the battleground, and at last characterizes a group's heritage in T20 cricket.

8.2 Integrating new players into the team culture

The most common way of coordinating new players into the group culture is a basic part of group working in any cricketing arrangement, especially in T20 associations like the Indian Head Association (IPL).

The mixture of new ability, frequently gained through sales, drafts, or moves, carries a powerful component to the group. Effective mix isn't just about absorbing new players into the crew; it includes encouraging a firm group culture, building fellowship, and adjusting individual yearnings to aggregate objectives.

At the beginning, the mix cycle starts with the appearance of new players into the group climate. Whether they are marquee signings, uncapped gifts, or experienced campaigners, every player brings an interesting arrangement of abilities, encounters, and characters to the group. The training staff, senior players, and group the board assume a urgent part in making an inviting environment, guaranteeing that fresh debuts feel esteemed and agreeable in their new environmental factors.

Correspondence is a key part in the combination cycle. Clear correspondence channels are laid out to convey the group's qualities, assumptions, and objectives. Skippers, mentors, and group pioneers articulate the group's vision, playing reasoning, and the jobs that players are supposed to satisfy. Furthermore, open lines of correspondence are empowered, permitting new players to communicate their thoughts, concerns, and assumptions. The incorporation interaction flourishes with straightforward and powerful correspondence.

Group building exercises, both on and off the field, structure an essential piece of the incorporation cycle. Instructional meetings, practice matches, and group holding exercises give open doors to players to manufacture associations, see each other's playing styles, and construct a feeling of solidarity. Off-field commitment, like group meals, excursions, or get-togethers, add to establishing a loose and harmonious climate where players can collaborate past the cricketing domain.

The mentorship framework assumes a critical part in directing new players through the combination cycle. Senior players or coaches inside the group assume on the liability of offering backing, exhortation, and bits of knowledge to rookies. This mentorship dynamic guides in adjusting new players to the group culture, furnishing them with a go-to hotspot for questions, and working with a smoother change into the crew. The mentorship framework cultivates a feeling of having a place and speeds up the coordination of new players.

Understanding and regarding variety is a foundation of fruitful incorporation. Cricket crews are in many cases a mixture of societies, dialects, and cricketing foundations. Embracing this variety enhances the group culture, establishing a climate where players gain from one another's cricketing encounters and social subtleties. The reconciliation cycle empowers an appreciation for variety, cultivating a feeling of solidarity chasing shared targets.

The training staff assumes a crucial part in adjusting new players to the group's playing reasoning and key goals. Instructing meetings include refining individual abilities as well as giving a comprehension of the group's strategic subtleties. New players are taught in the group's approaches, methodologies for explicit match situations, and the job they are supposed to play inside the bigger system. The instructing staff goes about as a scaffold between individual gifts and aggregate achievement.

The group's administration, frequently encapsulated by the chief, establishes the vibe for the mix cycle. Commanders assume a double part of on-field pioneers and off-field forces to be reckoned with, forming the group's way of life and encouraging solidarity. Their authority style, relational abilities, and capacity to construct compatibility contribute fundamentally to how new players absorb into the group. The combination interaction flourishes under commanders who focus on inclusivity, support, and a common feeling of direction.

Setting clear assumptions and jobs is principal in the combination cycle. New players need an exhaustive comprehension of their obligations, both on and off the field. Whether it's a batsman's job in securing the innings or a bowler's liability in unambiguous match circumstances, lucidity on jobs guarantees that players can contribute really and adjust their singular endeavors to the group's goals. The combination interaction benefits from a distinct design that permits players to figure out their specialty inside the group dynamic.

The group culture stresses an aggregate mentality, where individual achievement is entwined with the group's prosperity. Acknowledgment and festivity of individual accomplishments add to a positive group climate. At the point when new players make significant commitments, their endeavors are recognized and celebrated, building up the possibility that everybody's prosperity adds to the general outcome of the group. This approach encourages a feeling of shared achievement and reinforces group solidarity.

In the hyper-serious climate of T20 associations, the joining system likewise includes overseeing player assumptions. The fervor and expectation encompassing marquee signings or arising gifts can prompt increased assumptions. Offsetting these assumptions with the real factors of group elements, vital necessities, and the requirement for coordinated effort is fundamental. Overseeing assumptions establishes a climate where players center around adding to the group's prosperity as opposed to individual achievements.

The combination cycle stretches out past the playing XI to remember players for the seat or in the stores. Each individual from the crew assumes a part in making a durable group culture. The training staff guarantees that players on the edges stay connected with, spurred, and prepared to step in when called upon. The mix interaction is comprehensive, incorporating the whole crew and encouraging a feeling of aggregate reason.

Group gatherings, procedure meetings, and strategic conversations become discussions for cooperation and thought trade during the coordination interaction. New players are urged to contribute their points of view, bits of knowledge, and ideas. This comprehensive methodology advances the group's essential conversations as well as enables new players to feel esteemed and fundamental to the dynamic interaction. The coordination cycle flourishes with a culture of aggregate information and shared proprietorship.

The mix of new players into the group culture is a continuous cycle that develops with each match, practice meeting, and group association. Commanders and mentors give close consideration to the elements inside the crew, distinguishing regions for development, and tending to any worries or difficulties that might emerge. The mix cycle is definitely not a one-time occasion; it requires consistent exertion, flexibility, and a guarantee to supporting a positive group climate.

The mentorship framework, presented prior in the coordination cycle, keeps on assuming a vital part as the season advances. Tutors offer direction on dealing with the tensions of T20 cricket, overseeing assumptions, and exploring the subtleties of the association. They become comrades for new players, offering a help framework that stretches out past cricketing exhortation to individual prosperity. The mentorship dynamic reinforces as the season unfurls, adding to the supported reconciliation of new players.

The fruitful coordination of new players is many times thought about in field exhibitions. As the season advances, new players start to track down their beat, comprehend their jobs all the more naturally, and contribute genuinely to the group's prosperity. The reconciliation cycle is approved when new players consistently mix into the group's texture, displaying their abilities inside the aggregate structure and adding profundity to the crew.

Off-field commitments likewise become vital to the incorporation interaction. Players take part in local area drives, noble cause occasions, and social obligation attempts as a component of the group's more extensive effort. The combination cycle reaches out past the limits of the cricket field, accentuating the job of players as envoys of the group's qualities and the soul of the game.

Celebrating group achievements and shared encounters turns into a sign of effective mix. Whether it's a pivotal success, a paramount presentation, or a critical group accomplishment, these minutes add to a common story that ties players together. The combination interaction isn't just about adjusting to a group; it's tied in with turning into a necessary piece of the group's excursion and adding to its aggregate heritage.

8.3 Initial challenges and successes for newly formed squads

The development of another cricket crew, whether in homegrown associations or worldwide rivalries, is a dynamic and complex cycle that includes different difficulties and victories. The underlying stage establishes the vibe for the group's excursion, enveloping the mixture of players, the foundation of group elements, and the route of early obstacles. Understanding the elements of recently shaped crews reveals insight into the complexities of building a strong unit that can conquer difficulties and make progress in the cutthroat scene of cricket.

One of the essential difficulties looked by recently shaped crews is the coordination of different gifts into a strong unit. Players from various foundations, societies, and playing styles should rapidly adjust to a common group culture. This challenge is especially clear in T20 associations like the Indian Head Association (IPL), where groups are much of the time a blend of worldwide and homegrown players. Overcoming any issues between prepared campaigners and arising gifts requires viable correspondence, group building exercises, and a steady group climate.

The determination of group pioneers, including the commander and instructing staff, is a vital part of the underlying stage for recently shaped crews. The chief establishes the vibe for the group with their administration style, key keenness, and capacity to rouse players. Mentors assume an essential part in forming the group's playing reasoning, giving strategic direction, and cultivating a positive group culture. The test lies in adjusting the authority vision to the yearnings and capacities of the players, making an agreeable and successful administration dynamic.

The foundation of group elements is one more test that recently framed crews wrestle with in the beginning phases. Grasping the qualities, shortcomings, and playing styles of individual players is fundamental for creating a reasonable group. The test lies in distinguishing player jobs, improving group mixes, and encouraging a feeling of brotherhood and common comprehension among crew individuals. Group building exercises, practice meetings, and match reproductions become basic apparatuses in this cycle, assisting players with gelling both on and off the field.

The early matches of a recently framed crew frequently act as a litmus test for its cohesiveness and versatility. The test lies in deciphering the well thought out courses of action and group elements examined off the field into successful on-field exhibitions. Players should rapidly adjust to match situations, grasp the subtleties of one another's down, and show versatility despite challenges. Early triumphs, whether concerning individual exhibitions or group triumphs, assume a pivotal part in building certainty and setting the direction for the season.

Progress in the early matches is frequently attached to the adequacy of the group's procedures and strategic keenness. The training staff assumes a key part in making an interpretation of masterful courses of action into on-field strategies. Choices with respect to batting orders, bowling pivots, and field positions are basic in enhancing the group's presentation. Progress in executing these strategic plans adds to positive outcomes as well as imparts a feeling of conviction and union inside the crew.

While early victories are empowering, recently framed crews definitely experience mishaps and difficulties. One of the normal obstacles is the variation to match conditions, particularly in associations where groups play across different scenes with various pitches and aspects. The test lies in rapidly understanding the attributes of each playing surface, adjusting playing techniques likewise, and limiting the effect of outside factors like atmospheric conditions.

Wounds and player accessibility issues present huge difficulties for recently framed crews. The profundity of the crew, especially the seat strength, is tried when central members are inaccessible because of wounds or different responsibilities. The test for the group the executives is to have alternate courses of action set up, sustain major areas of strength for a seat, and guarantee that the crew stays versatile notwithstanding surprising unlucky deficiencies. The capacity to explore through these difficulties frequently decides the versatility and profundity of a recently shaped crew.

Group science and correspondence elements are tried under tension circumstances, particularly in firmly challenged matches or high-stakes experiences. The test lies in keeping up with viable correspondence channels, keeping away from misconceptions, and encouraging a feeling of solidarity during testing minutes. The initiative gathering, including the chief and senior players, assumes a critical part in keeping the group centered, imparting certainty, and guaranteeing that players support each other through the two triumphs and difficulties.

The elements of group choice and player pivots present difficulties for recently shaped crews. Mentors and selectors should find some kind of harmony among consistency and versatility, guaranteeing that the best playing XI is handled for each match. The test lies in overseeing player responsibilities, upgrading the crew's exhibition in light of resistance qualities, and rolling out essential improvements when required. The beginning stage fills in as a proving ground for figuring out player mixes and tweaking choice procedures.

Progress in a cricketing setting isn't exclusively characterized by match results yet in addition by the improvement of individual players inside the crew. The underlying stage gives an open door to players, particularly arising gifts, to feature their abilities and set up a good foundation for themselves as vital supporters. Examples of overcoming adversity inside the crew, whether it's a youthful player making a forward leap or a carefully prepared campaigner conveying significant exhibitions, add to the general achievement and personality of the group.

The job of group the board in encouraging a positive group culture is foremost during the underlying stage. Establishing a climate where players feel esteemed, upheld, and roused is fundamental for long haul achievement. The test for group the executives lies in finding some kind of harmony among discipline and adaptability, imparting a feeling of pride among players, and guaranteeing that the group culture is comprehensive and strong despite challenges.

As the underlying difficulties are explored, the triumphs of recently framed crews become venturing stones until the end of the time. Early triumphs add to a positive group outlook, gather speed, and make a feeling of conviction inside the crew. The test lies in keeping up with consistency and expanding on these early victories, guaranteeing that the group advances and develops further with each match.

The foundation of a triumphant culture is a critical accomplishment for recently shaped crews. It goes past individual exhibitions or match results and includes the development of an outlook where players are propelled to do everything they possibly can in each game. Achievement is estimated with regards to prizes as well as in the strength, versatility, and solidarity that characterize the group's personality. The test for recently shaped crews is to engrain this triumphant culture right off the bat in the season and support it all through the mission.

Early triumphs add to the group's remaining in the association or competition, affecting the race for season finisher compartments and title conflict. The test for recently shaped crews is to explore the intricacies of competition designs, point frameworks, and net run rates really. The capacity to comprehend the essential ramifications of each match and settle on informed choices becomes urgent chasing after season finisher capabilities and, at last, title greatness.

Group holding and the improvement of a solid emotionally supportive network are vital parts of the outcome of recently framed crews. Whether it's the care staff, establishment proprietors, or the energetic fanbase, a firm help structure adds to the group's prosperity. The test for crews is to outfit this aggregate energy, draw motivation from the help they get, and make a feeling of local area that reaches out past the battleground.

Chapter 9

Triumphs and Heartbreaks

Wins and heartbreaks comprise the profound embroidered artwork of cricket, winding around together stories of thrilling triumphs and horrible losses. In the powerful universe of the game, where the pendulum swings between upbeat festivals and impactful reflections, each victory and deplorability makes a permanent imprint on players, groups, and fans the same. Investigating these ups and downs uncovers the significant effect of cricket on people and the aggregate mind of cricketing countries.

Wins on the cricket field are likened to ensembles that resound with the aggregate heartbeat of a group and its allies. Triumphs, whether exhaustive or hard-battled, inspire celebration and a feeling of achievement. The happiness of a victorious second frequently rises above the limit ropes, restricting players and fans in a common festival of progress. At these times cricket turns into a bringing together power, encouraging a deep satisfaction and having a place among the individuals who wear the group's tones or cheer from the stands.

World Cup wins stand as the zenith of cricketing accomplishments, scratching snapshots of greatness into the archives of the game's set of experiences.

The Cricket World Cup, held like clockwork, is a worldwide display where countries strive for matchless quality. Winning the World Cup is an incredible accomplishment, a demonstration of a group's expertise, strength, and capacity to perform under the most extreme tension. The close to home crescendo of lifting the prize before loving fans is an unmatched snapshot of win for players and a well-spring of persevering through pride for the cricketing countries they address.

With regards to homegrown associations like the Indian Head Association (IPL), wins are about flatware as well as about the excursion of recovery and strength. Groups that come back to life, conquer misfortunes, and secure the title represent the substance of win in T20 cricket. The rowdy festivals, the dazed fans, and seeing players lolling in the brilliance of their prosperity make an electric climate that resounds across arenas and TV screens.

In any case, wins in cricket are not restricted to the amazing phases of World Cups and T20 associations. Test cricket, with its laborious fights north of five days, frequently creates triumphs that are slow-cooked and hard-procured. Seeing players, actually and intellectually depleted in the wake of defeating the difficulties presented by the longest organization, implies the profundity of their victories. Whether it's a notable series win on unfamiliar soil or a last-pant triumph in a firmly challenged Test match, these victories in whites convey a particular and persevering through beguile.

However, interweaved with the rapture of wins are the heartbreaks that add a powerful aspect to the cricketing story. Routs in vital matches, close to misses, and the desolation of missing the mark in quest for greatness make an embroidery of heartbreaks that bring out sympathy and versatility. For each group that lifts a prize, there are others that should wrestle with the severe taste of rout, encouraging a feeling of contemplation and the assurance to rise once more.

World Cup heartbreaks resound with cricket fans across the globe, epitomizing the brutal magnificence of game. The last snapshots of a firmly challenged World Cup match, particularly in the restricted overs designs, can swing among delight and distress. Whether it's the grievousness of losing in a sensational Over or missing the mark in a strained run pursue, these minutes become scratched in the recollections of players and fans the same. The tears, the reassuring embraces, and the sad strolls back to the structure uncover the human side of cricket, where win and misfortune coincide on the most terrific stage.

In homegrown T20 associations, where the organization is intended for un-conventionality and nail-gnawing gets done, heartbreaks become a natural piece of the story. Groups that overwhelm the association stage can wind up on some unacceptable side of fortune in knockout matches, surrendering to the tension of abrupt passing experiences. Seeing down and out players and broke dreams makes a glaring difference to the richness of win, showing the fine edges that characterize achievement and catastrophe in the speedy universe of T20 cricket.

Test cricket, with its nuanced and frequently long fights, produces heartbreaks that cut profound into the cricketing soul. A bold rearguard exertion that misses the mark, a misconception that prompts rout in the last meeting, or the failure to pursue down an unassuming objective on the fifth day — this large number of situations evoke a feeling of deplorability that is remarkable to the longest configuration. The sluggish disentangling of a group's fortunes, combined with the certainty of rout, tests the flexibility and character of players and leaves an enduring engraving on the cricketing story.

Individual exhibitions, both chivalrous and tragic, add to the close to home scene of wins and heartbreaks in cricket. Hundreds of years scored under massive strain, match-dominating bowling spells, and remarkable gets become parts of win that characterize a player's heritage. On the other hand, the distress of a duck in an essential innings, a dropped get that demonstrates expensive, or a delinquent conveyance in the last over of a nearby match makes individual heartbreaks that players should explore in the public eye.

The idea of 'what might have been' adds a layer of grievousness to cricketing stories. Snapshots of splendor that are eclipsed by a definitive result, choices that explosion, or botched open doors that change the direction of a match — all add to the self-contradicting nature of the game. Cricket, with its inborn vulnerabilities and the chance of defining moments in each meeting, fits a consistent exchange among wins and heartbreaks.

The job of administration becomes amplified in snapshots of win and misfortune. Commanders are not simply strategists; they are personal anchors directing the boat through the ups and downs of a cricketing effort. The rapture of lifting a prize or the obligation of supporting crushed players after a tragic misfortune falls unequivocally on the shoulders of skippers. Their capacity to lead with elegance in win and strength in misfortune characterizes their heritage in the game.

For fans, wins and heartbreaks in cricket are profoundly private encounters that bring out a rollercoaster of feelings. The thunder of satisfaction when a most loved player stirs things up around town runs, the deep breath of help when a bowler takes a vital wicket, or the common frustration when a group misses the mark — all add to the close to home venture that fans fill the game. Cricket, with its ability to join networks and rise above borders, turns into a common excursion of wins and heartbreaks for fans all over the planet.

The stories of wins and heartbreaks stretch out past the battleground to the more extensive setting of cricket as a social peculiarity. Famous minutes, whether it's Kapil Dev lifting the 1983 World Cup or Ben Stirs up's chivalrous innings in the 2019 World Cup last, become piece of the shared perspective of cricketing countries. These minutes characterize cricketing heritages as well as act as social standards that reverberate through ages.

In the period of establishment based T20 associations, the victories and heartbreaks of individual players become weaved with the personality of the groups they address. The dependability of fans, the enthusiasm of neighborhood networks, and the electric environment in pressed arenas enhance the close to home stakes of each match. Wins are praised as common triumphs, while heartbreaks are imparted troubles that fans convey to enduring help for their groups.

The stories of wins and heartbreaks in cricket likewise highlight the transient idea of accomplishment and disappointment. A victorious group in one season might confront heartbreaks in the following, as well as the other way around. The consistently developing nature of the game guarantees that no group or player is invulnerable to the profound rollercoaster that characterizes cricket. This capriciousness adds a layer of tension and fervor, keeping fans as eager and anxious as ever all through a cricketing season.

The division of wins and heartbreaks makes cricket a profoundly full and human game. It reflects life's ups and downs, offering snapshots of unrestrained bliss and showing flexibility notwithstanding difficulty. The close to home venture of players, the initiative difficulties for chiefs, and the aggregate insight of fans make a rich embroidery that goes past the measurements and scorecards. Cricket, with its victories and heartbreaks, rises above the limits of a simple game, turning into a common excursion that interfaces individuals across societies and ages.

9.1 Analyzing the success stories of teams post-auction

The post-sell off progressively ease in cricket is a time of extreme examination, expectation, and key making arrangements for groups taking part in associations like the Indian Chief Association (IPL). Following the high-stakes closeout, where establishments contend to construct their crews, the ensuing time frame is set apart by a careful evaluation of player mixes, group elements, and vital qualities. Examining the examples of overcoming adversity of groups post-closeout divulges the complexities of transforming a different arrangement of players into a firm and cutthroat unit.

Effective groups post-sell off are many times described by an obvious group methodology that lines up with the establishment's general vision. The cycle starts with a careful assessment of the group's assets and shortcomings, both from the past season and considering the progressions made during the sale. This reflection sets the establishment for distinguishing the particular player profiles expected to support the group's presentation across batting, bowling, and handling divisions.

One critical part of post-closeout investigation is the acknowledgment of the establishment's marquee players and their possible effect in group elements.

Marquee players, frequently obtained through high-profile offers, are supposed to be the key parts around whom the group's technique rotates. Their jobs stretch out past on-field commitments; marquee players act as ministers for the establishment, drawing consideration, and fans to make a brand character. Fruitful groups influence the star force of their marquee players to upgrade both on-field execution and off-field perceivability.

In the IPL, where the T20 design requests a sensitive harmony between power hitters, solid batsmen, and talented bowlers, groups fastidiously evaluate the qualities and shortcomings of their playing XI. Post-closeout investigation includes a granular assessment of batting orders, bowling blends, and the flexibility of players to adjust to various match situations. Groups decisively select players who can flourish in unambiguous jobs, for example, openers who can furnish dangerous beginnings or bowlers with a talent for taking wickets in the center overs.

The meaning of all-rounders in T20 cricket enhances the significance of post-sell off examination. Groups look for players who can contribute with both bat and ball, giving adaptability in group piece and vital choices during matches. The examples of overcoming adversity of groups frequently include keen picks of all-rounders who can turn the course of a game with a quickfire innings, an essential leap forward, or a game-evolving spell. The capacity to recognize and get significant all-rounders is a sign of powerful post-sell off investigation.

Key dynamic post-closeout reaches out to the ID of potential match-champs, frequently alluded to as 'X-factor' players. These are people with the capacity to convey game-evolving exhibitions, whether through unstable batting, unplayable bowling spells, or athletic handling. Effective groups post-closeout perceive these X-factor players as well as establish a climate that permits them to put themselves out there unreservedly on the field, releasing their capability to swing matches in the group's approval.

The organization of the crew as far as experienced players and arising gifts is a vital part of post-closeout examples of overcoming adversity. Groups work out some kind of harmony between prepared campaigners who bring initiative, security, and game dominating experience, and youthful gifts with the craving and dynamism to leave an imprint. The mentorship and mix of arising gifts into the group culture become necessary parts of post-sell off methodologies, guaranteeing an agreeable mix of youth and experience.

Establishment think tanks likewise dig into the complexities of player blends, taking into account the collaboration between various playing styles and ranges of abilities. For instance, the harmony between forceful stroke-producers and gatherers in the batting arrangement, or the blend of speed and twist choices in the bowling division, is painstakingly aligned during post-sell off examination. Groups look for an amicable mix that boosts collaboration and limits likely shortcomings in unambiguous match conditions.

Information driven experiences assume an essential part in post-closeout examination, with groups progressively depending on investigation to illuminate their systems. Measurable measurements, player execution information from past seasons, and progressed examination apparatuses add to informed navigation. Effective groups utilize information investigators to decipher patterns, evaluate player structure, and distinguish designs that can illuminate on-field methodologies. The joining of information driven bits of knowledge into post-closeout investigation is an impression of the developing idea of current cricket the executives.

While individual exhibitions are critical, group science and brotherhood arise as central places of post-closeout examples of overcoming adversity. Groups put resources into making a positive and durable group culture where players team up, convey successfully, and fashion solid bonds on and off the field. The administration bunch, including the skipper and training staff, assumes a focal part in cultivating a group climate that energizes common help, shared goals, and a feeling of aggregate possession.

Post-sell off examples of overcoming adversity likewise feature the flexibility and vital insight of groups during the competition. The capacity to change playing blends in light of resistance qualities, match conditions, and strategic subtleties turns into a critical calculate supporting achievement. Groups that show adaptability in their systems, pursue keen in-game choices, and adjust to developing difficulties frequently wind up on the triumphant side of post-sell off stories.

The job of training staff and backing faculty in post-closeout achievement couldn't possibly be more significant. Groups with experienced mentors, specific care staff, and a hearty private cabin framework are better prepared to outfit the capability of their players. Training staff work on refining abilities, giving strategic direction, and guaranteeing that players are genuinely and intellectually ready for the requests of a thorough competition. The examples of overcoming adversity of groups post-sell off frequently feature the in the background commitments of the training arrangement.

Initiative turns into a key part in making an interpretation of post-sell off procedures into on-field achievement. Chiefs, frequently the substance of the establishment, assume a double part as essential masterminds and inspirations. Fruitful pioneers impart trust in their players, pursue canny strategic choices during matches, and show others how its done through their on-field exhibitions. Post-sell off examples of overcoming adversity are frequently interlaced with the commander's capacity to move, adjust, and explore the group through the recurring pattern of a competition.

The effect of outer variables, like wounds and player accessibility, is one more layer of post-closeout examination. Groups that really oversee player responsibilities, have alternate courses of action for startling misfortunes, and influence crew profundity frequently passage better even with unanticipated difficulties.

The capacity to explore through the intricacies of a long competition, particularly in associations like the IPL, is a demonstration of a group's versatility and flexibility post-closeout.

Methodologies for overseeing player revolutions, particularly in consecutive apparatuses, assume an essential part in post-closeout examples of overcoming adversity. Groups survey responsibility the board, structure contemplations, and resistance matchups to enhance player blends for various matches. Fruitful groups find some kind of harmony among congruity and turn, guaranteeing that central members are refreshed when required while keeping up with the group's strategic advantage.

Post-sell off examples of overcoming adversity likewise mirror the effect of fan support and the climate made in arenas or virtual spaces. Establishments that develop an energetic fanbase, draw in with allies through different drives, and make a dynamic group culture frequently experience a positive criticism circle. The energy produced by intense fan support turns into a main thrust for players, encouraging a climate where they feel an awareness of others' expectations to convey accomplishment on the field.

Examples of overcoming adversity post-closeout come full circle in season finisher capabilities and, for the lucky few, title wins. Groups that explore the gathering stages effectively, grandstand flexibility in knockout experiences, and adapt to the situation in high-pressure circumstances cut an enduring heritage. The celebration of arriving at the end of the season games and the happiness of bringing home the title epitomize a definitive targets of post-sell off systems.

9.2 Examining the reasons behind underperforming teams

Looking at the explanations for failing to meet expectations groups in cricket, especially in high-stakes associations like the Indian Head Association (IPL), reveals a complicated transaction of elements that add to their battles on the field. While each season observers examples of overcoming adversity, there are groups that wind up grieving at the lower part of the table, incapable to make an interpretation of potential into steady execution. Diving into the complexities of underperformance reveals insight into key components, going from key stumbles to inner difficulties, that ruin groups from understanding their maximum capacity.

One of the principal factors adding to underperformance is the insufficiency of the group's essential system, both during the sale and all through the season. Groups that neglect to adjust their techniques to the remarkable requests of T20 cricket wind up in a difficult situation. This misalignment can appear in the determination of players who don't complete one another qualities, making uneven characters in the crew. Deficient accentuation on key perspectives like power-hitting, adaptable bowling choices, and key adaptability frequently leaves groups unfit to explore the difficulties presented by unique T20 designs.

Key stumbles during the bartering frequently set the vibe for failing to meet expectations groups. Unfortunate player choice, either due to exaggerating specific abilities or neglecting basic viewpoints, can prompt an absence of equilibrium in the crew. For example, a group that neglects to get dependable center request batsmen or needs profundity in its bowling assets might battle in pivotal match circumstances. The outcomes of these essential mistakes become clear during the season, as groups wrestle with the repercussions of imperfect closeout techniques.

The creation of the administration bunch, including the skipper and training staff, assumes a urgent part in deciding a group's prosperity or underperformance. Powerless or incapable authority can saturate the whole crew, influencing dynamic on and off the field. Skippers who battle to move certainty, make vital mistakes, or neglect to make a positive group culture can coincidentally add to the underperformance of their groups. Also, training staff that misses the mark on mastery to tweak player abilities, devise compelling techniques, and support group elements might fuel the difficulties looked by failing to meet expectations groups.

Group elements and unseen fits of turmoil inside the crew arise as huge supporters of underperformance. An absence of union, correspondence breakdowns, or character conflicts among players can make a poisonous air that hampers on-field exhibitions. Effective groups frequently focus on group building exercises, encourage a comprehensive culture, and guarantee that players feel esteemed and upheld. Failing to meet expectations groups, then again, may wrestle with issues connected with inner self conflicts, independence, or an absence of aggregate liability, prompting sub-standard outcomes.

Wounds and player inaccessibility structure one more layer of difficulties that failing to meet expectations groups should battle with. The shortfall of vital participants because of wounds or global responsibilities can weaken group blends and power dependence on untested substitutions. Failing to meet expectations groups might end up poorly ready to deal with these mishaps, coming up short on the crew profundity or alternate courses of action expected to explore an exhausting competition plan. Conversely, fruitful groups proactively address these difficulties, guaranteeing that the crew stays versatile and versatile to unexpected conditions.

The underutilization or bungle of players inside the crew contributes fundamentally to underperformance. Groups that neglect to perceive and tackle the maximum capacity of their players, either by sending them in sub-par jobs or not giving satisfactory open doors, risk wasting ability. For example, a power-hitter reliably batting lower in the request or an expert bowler underutilized in unambiguous match conditions can sabotage the group's general presentation. Effective groups skillfully send players in jobs that augment their assets and adjust techniques in view of the powerful necessities of each match.

Key rigidity during matches addresses a basic variable behind the underperformance of groups. In the speedy climate of T20 cricket, where match circumstances can change quickly, unbending strategies can demonstrate impeding. Groups that stick determinedly to biased techniques without adjusting to advancing match situations frequently wind up outsmarted by additional adaptable rivals. Effective groups display the capacity to peruse the game, make continuous changes, and gain by the shortcomings of their rivals, while failing to meet expectations groups might battle to show such versatility.

The effect of outside factors, for example, horrible match conditions, climate interferences, or a difficult timetable, further intensifies the difficulties looked by failing to meet expectations groups. While effective groups explore these outer factors with versatility and flexibility, failing to meet expectations groups might capitulate to the extra tensions and disturbances. The failure to deal with antagonistic conditions can additionally subvert the certainty and execution of groups battling to track down their beat.

An absence of viable correspondence and key arrangement between establishment proprietors, group the board, and players addresses one more feature of underperformance. Establishment proprietors who apply unnecessary effect in group choice, subvert the power of the training staff, or establish a climate of vulnerability can add to an absence of steadiness inside the group. Fruitful groups lay out an unmistakable order and correspondence channel, permitting the training staff to work with independence and settle on choices in view of cricketing merit as opposed to outside pressures.

Monetary contemplations and financial plan imperatives can likewise affect the presentation of groups in associations with pay covers, like the IPL. Failing to meet expectations groups might battle to work out some kind of harmony between dispensing assets to marquee players and building a balanced crew. Overspending on a couple of headliners to the detriment of crew profundity or underrating the significance of significant worth for-cash signings can prompt uneven characters. Fruitful groups deal with their financial plans wisely, making key speculations that upgrade the general strength and profundity of the crew.

At times, failing to meet expectations groups might wrestle with an absence of congruity in their methodology, habitually evolving skippers, training staff, or group pieces. This flimsiness can disturb the improvement of group science, upset vital preparation, and dissolve the certainty of players. Effective groups, then again, focus on steadiness and progression, permitting players and training staff to construct connections and foster a mutual perspective of the group's goals over different seasons.

The idea of the competition design, particularly in associations like the IPL, where groups play countless matches in a moderately brief period, adds a layer of physical and mental weakness. Failing to meet expectations groups might battle to oversee player jobs successfully, prompting burnout, loss of structure, or expanded powerlessness to wounds.

Effective groups execute pivot techniques, rest vital participants decisively, and guarantee a harmony between serious power and player prosperity all through the competition.

The shortfall of a strong exploring and ability distinguishing proof framework can frustrate failing to meet expectations groups in finding and supporting arising gifts. Effective groups put resources into complete exploring organizations, guaranteeing that they stay side by side of promising youthful players who might possibly reinforce the crew. Failing to meet expectations groups might pass up uncovering unlikely treasures, passing on holes in their crew arrangement and neglecting to profit by the capability of arising gifts.

Emergency the executives and the capacity to bounce back from mishaps are basic credits that failing to meet expectations groups frequently need. While each group faces difficulties during a competition, those that can explore emergencies successfully, gain from disappointments, and make key changes return more grounded. Effective groups view mishaps as learning valuable open doors, adjusting their systems and building up a versatile group culture that encourages a positive mentality.

The absence of fan commitment and support can likewise add to the battles of failing to meet expectations groups. An unsettled fanbase, disappointed by reliable underperformance, may separate from supporting the group, influencing the general air and spirit. Interestingly, effective groups develop an energetic fan finishing reliable exhibitions, local area commitment, and a dynamic group culture that reverberates with allies.

9.3 The role of auction decisions in determining on-field success

The job of sale choices in deciding on-field progress in cricket, particularly in high-profile associations like the Indian Head Association (IPL), is a multi-layered and basic part of a group's excursion. The sale fills in as the door for establishments to collect their crews, introducing an essential combat zone where choices made can have extensive results in the group's presentation all through the competition. Digging into the complexities of sale elements, player determinations, and group building methodologies uncovers the essential job these choices play in forming the fate of a group on the field.

At the core of the sale cycle is the choice of players, each bringing a novel arrangement of abilities, experience, and expected game evolving skills. The outcome of a group relies on the capacity to get players who fit into the group's essential system as well as have the flexibility and versatility expected in the unique T20 design. Closeout choices are, consequently, instrumental in deciding the quality and sythesis of a group's playing XI.

One of the crucial parts of closeout choices is the distinguishing proof of marquee players — the people who are supposed to be the foundations of the group's prosperity. Establishments put significant assets and take part in offering battles to get marquee players, frequently global cricketing whizzes or demonstrated T20 subject matter experts. The choice to target explicit marquee players mirrors the group's essential needs, marking goals, and the craving to have persuasive figures around whom the group can rotate.

The closeout methodology likewise includes surveying the group's prerequisites across various jobs and ranges of abilities. Groups should figure out some kind of harmony between power-hitters, dependable batsmen, wicket-taking bowlers, and spry defenders. The choices made during the bartering to get players who satisfy these jobs add to the general group balance, guaranteeing that the crew is exceptional to deal with different match circumstances and resistance challenges.

The offering system itself is a high-stakes try where key intuition, speedy direction, and monetary reasonability become an integral factor. Establishments participate in extraordinary exchanges, utilizing a mix of examination, investigation, and impulse to outsmart contenders and secure the administrations of wanted players. Sell off choices are, in this way, an impression of a group's capacity to peruse the market, evaluate player esteems precisely, and make quick offers inside the imperatives of financial plan contemplations.

Financial plan contemplations structure a basic part of closeout choices, particularly in associations like the IPL where pay covers limit the sum a group can spend on player acquisitions. Successful spending plan the board is urgent for groups to work out some kind of harmony between getting marquee players, filling key positions, and keeping up with crew profundity. The choice to distribute assets reasonably, keeping away from overreliance on a couple of costly players while guaranteeing sufficient assets for a balanced crew, is demonstrative of a group's monetary judiciousness.

The job of group proprietors and the board in closeout choices couldn't possibly be more significant. Proprietors frequently set the vibe for the group's methodology, association in the sale cycle, and readiness to pursue striking choices. How they might interpret the game, arrangement with the instructing staff, and obligation to giving the important assets fundamentally influence the group's capacity to settle on successful sale choices. Effective groups benefit from proprietors who bring an essential vision, cricketing discernment, and long haul obligation to the table.

Closeout choices likewise spin around the determination of arising gifts — uncapped players who can possibly become future stars. Recognizing and supporting youthful, promising players is a demonstration of a group's premonition and obligation to working for what's to come. The choice to put resources into arising abilities fortifies the group's seat strength as well as adds to the general intensity and maintainability of the crew.

Vital prescience assumes a critical part in closeout choices, especially in expecting future patterns, understanding the developing elements of T20 cricket, and anticipating long haul achievement. Fruitful groups display a proactive way to deal with exploring arising gifts, distinguishing players with neglected potential, and pursuing choices that line up with the direction of the game. The capacity to expect shifts in player values, group systems, and the requests of the organization positions a group for supported accomplishment past individual seasons.

The closeout fills in as a stage for groups to address explicit shortcomings or build up solid areas inside the crew. Closeout choices, in this manner, include a fastidious examination of the group's presentation in past seasons, distinguishing holes in the playing XI, and making designated acquisitions to support those viewpoints. Whether it's fortifying the center request, adding profundity to the bowling office, or getting a dependable wicketkeeper-batsman, these choices add to the group's by and large essential development.

Group building procedures during the sale stretch out past individual player choices to the production of a strong and synergistic unit. Closeout choices that encourage a positive group culture, advance brotherhood among players, and guarantee an agreeable mix of experienced campaigners and arising gifts establish the groundwork for on-field achievement. The elements of group science, frequently impacted by sell off choices, assume a significant part in molding the aggregate personality and strength of the crew.

The choice to put resources into all-rounders, players who contribute with both bat and ball, is an essential move that upgrades a group's adaptability and versatility. Sell off choices to get significant all-rounders — the people who can turn the course of a game with both their batting and abilities to bowl — become pivotal in the T20 design. Fruitful groups perceive the worth of all-rounders in giving equilibrium to the playing XI and guaranteeing key choices in different match situations.

The job of training staff in affecting closeout choices can't be ignored. Mentors, with their cricketing skill, vital experiences, and comprehension of player elements, work together with group the board to plan closeout methodologies. Their contributions during the sale cycle, particularly in surveying player capacities, checking group necessities, and adjusting choices to the group's playing style, contribute fundamentally to the outcome of closeout choices.

The worldwide versus homegrown player balance is one more key thought in closeout choices. Groups should pursue choices on the blend of abroad and neighborhood players in light of the essential prerequisites, group elements, and the strategic requests of the configuration. Effective groups find some kind of harmony, utilizing the qualities of global stars while sustaining and displaying the gifts of homegrown players.

Closeout choices are additionally impacted by the configuration explicit requests of T20 cricket. The capacity to recognize players who flourish in the quick moving, high-pressure nature of T20 matches turns into a basic element. Groups should evaluate a player's range of abilities as well as their personality, versatility to various match circumstances, and capacity to perform under extreme examination. Sell off choices that line up with the novel requests of T20 cricket position a group for outcome in the quick and eccentric organization.

The bartering, being a dynamic and cutthroat climate, requests flexibility and speedy navigation. Fruitful groups display spryness in their dynamic cycle, answering actually to evolving situations, and benefiting from potential open doors as they emerge. The capacity to remain created under tension, pursue informed choices on the fly, and adjust procedures in light of developing closeout elements is a sign of groups that succeed in the bartering room.

The effect of closeout choices stretches out past the quick player determinations to the more extensive goals of establishment proprietors. Groups with an unmistakable vision, lined up with the ethos of the establishment, and focused on building a maintainable cricketing heritage settle on choices that reverberate with their drawn out objectives. Fruitful groups center around quick accomplishment as well as focus on the foundation of a solid brand character, fan commitment, and local area outreach through their closeout choices.

Key unions and coordinated efforts with different groups or players, frequently started during the sale, likewise add to a group's prosperity. The choice to frame associations, influence collaborations, or participate in player trades mirrors a group's capacity to explore the complexities of the cricketing environment. Fruitful groups perceive the worth of cooperative endeavors in building an upper hand and upgrading the general strength of the crew.

The sale choices made by a group impact not exclusively its on-field achievement yet additionally its attractiveness and fan bid. Fruitful groups influence the star force of marquee players, make promoting efforts that resound with fans, and fabricate major areas of strength for a media presence. The choice to put resources into players who succeed on the field as well as add to the establishment's off-field perceivability is an essential move that upgrades the group's general allure.

9.4 Recap of key themes and insights

As we dig into a complete recap of key subjects and experiences encompassing the unpredictable universe of Indian Head Association (IPL) barters, groups, strategies, and wins, it becomes clear that the excursion from the sale space to the battleground is a diverse embroidery woven with vital choices, dynamic player elements, and the tireless quest for progress.

IPL Sales: Revealing the Show

The IPL barters are an arresting scene where establishments take part in wild offering battles to gather their fantasy crews. The closeout elements include a sensitive harmony between getting marquee players, tending to group prerequisites, and overseeing spending plans sensibly. The marquee players, frequently worldwide cricketing symbols or demonstrated T20 trained professionals, become the central focuses around which groups construct their methodologies. The serious idea of the sale, described by extraordinary dealings and vital moves, makes way for the ensuing IPL season's account.

Development of IPL Sell-offs: A Short History

To comprehend the ongoing meaning of IPL barters, following their advancement over the course of the years is fundamental. The sales, which started as a way to lay out a level battleground among establishments, have changed into high-stakes occasions with extensive ramifications. From the early years when establishments were sorting out the subtleties of group working to the current time set apart by essential complexity, the IPL barters have reflected the always changing scene of T20 cricket.

The Bartering Field: Making way for Cricketing Theater

The bartering field itself is a performance center of dreams and vulnerabilities. Establishment proprietors, mentors, and specialists carefully plan their moves, shuffling between spending plan imperatives and the quest for star power. The choice of marquee players turns into an assertion of goal, mirroring a group's vision and desire. The elements of the closeout field shape the fortunes of individual players as well as establish the groundwork for the show that unfurls on the cricket field.

Setting the Stage: Scene and Environment

The scene and air of the sale add an additional layer of fervor to the procedures. Whether held in extravagant lodgings or clamoring halls, the sale scene turns into the focal point of cricketing systems. The discernible strain, the essential conversations among group proprietors, and the excitement of latest possible moment offers make a zapping climate. The decision of setting and the general climate add to the air of the closeout, raising it past a simple player securing process.

Sell off Elements and Rules: Exploring the Chessboard

Understanding the complexities of sale elements and rules is likened to exploring a chessboard where each move has results. The compensation cap forces monetary requirements, compelling groups to settle on essential conclusions about asset designation. The Option to Match (RTM) card presents an extra layer of system, permitting groups to hold central members. The maintenance and delivery strategies, combined with the uncapped player guidelines, make a complicated chessboard where groups should think a few maneuvers ahead to guarantee a fair and serious crew.

Key Partners: Establishment Proprietors, Mentors, and Players

The outcome of an IPL group is dependent upon the coordinated effort and cooperative energy among key partners — establishment proprietors, mentors, and players. Proprietors, frequently addressing a blend of business keenness and cricketing enthusiasm, set the essential vision for the group. Mentors bring strategic mastery and assume a urgent part in player improvement. Players, a definitive entertainers on the field, are the epitomes of a group's yearnings and systems. The agreeable cooperation between these partners is the bedrock of a fruitful IPL crusade.

Building the Outline: Pre-Closeout Arrangements

The pre-sell off stage is a pivotal period where establishments carefully make their plans for progress. The essential research organizations dig into player examinations, group prerequisites, and strategic subtleties. They evaluate the qualities and shortcomings from the past season, recognizing regions for development. The pre-closeout arrangements include an exhaustive comprehension of the market elements, player valuations, and potential objective acquisitions. This stage establishes the vibe for the resulting sell off methodologies and shapes the fate of the group.

Financial plan Contemplations and Group Systems: Difficult exercise

Financial plan contemplations structure the essence of closeout procedures, driving groups to figure out some kind of harmony between marquee signings and crew profundity. Establishments should be sharp in dispensing assets to get influence players while guaranteeing adequate assets for a balanced group. The capacity to oversee spending plans really reflects monetary reasonability, a quality fundamental for long haul manageability. Fruitful groups display a nuanced comprehension of the monetary limitations, utilizing their assets to construct imposing crews.

Job of Group Research organizations: Brains at Work

The job of group think tanks, containing proprietors, mentors, examiners, and planners, is similar to geniuses organizing a fabulous methodology. These scholarly engineers carefully plan player acquisitions, survey group elements, and devise strategic diagrams.

The collaboration between group proprietors and instructing staff is basic, cultivating a climate where cricketing choices are lined up with the all-encompassing vision. The capacity of the research organization to predict difficulties, adjust to evolving conditions, and pursue informed choices shapes the group's direction.

Marquee Players and Uber Offers: Symbols of the Bartering

Marquee players arise as the banner young men of the sale, drawing uber offers and turning into the highlights of group methodologies. The obtaining of marquee players stretches out past their on-field ability; it includes brand esteem, fan commitment, and the making of an unmistakable group personality. Uber offers for marquee players stand out as truly newsworthy as well as imply the forceful plan of establishments. The determination of marquee players is an essential move that goes past cricketing abilities, impacting the group's attractiveness and fan request.

Examination of Marquee Players: Past the Cricket Field

The investigation of marquee players goes past factual measurements; it digs into the intangibles that make them cricketing symbols. Past their batting midpoints or bowling strike rates, marquee players bring initiative characteristics, star power, and the capacity to deal with pressure circumstances. Establishments carefully evaluate the off-field credits of marquee players, taking into account their effect in group culture, fan commitment, and generally brand situating. The outcome of marquee players isn't only estimated in runs or wickets however in the comprehensive commitment to the group's account.

High-Profile Offering Wars and Record-Breaking Arrangements: Sale Vain behaviors

High-profile offering wars and record-breaking bargains are the embodiment of sale vain behaviors, enrapturing crowds and adding a layer of excitement to the procedures. Establishments participate in wild fights, pushing the limits of monetary judiciousness to get the administrations of desired players. The adrenaline-siphoning snapshots of offering wars and the happiness encompassing record-breaking bargains make permanent recollections in the personalities of fans. These scenes characterize the high-stakes nature of the IPL barters, where the quest for greatness comes along with some built-in costs.

Effect of Marquee Players in Group Creation and Fanbase: Past Runs and Wickets

The effect of marquee players rises above the mathematical insights of runs and wickets; it saturates the actual texture of group creation and fanbase devotion. Marquee players become the key parts around whom the group's methodologies spin. Their on-field heroics rouse partners, while their off-field charm makes an interface with fans. The faithfulness and close to home speculation of fans toward marquee players cultivate a feeling of having a place and dependability, transforming cricket into a social peculiarity past the limits of the battleground.

9.5 Reflection on the impact of IPL Auctions on the league

The Indian Head Association (IPL) Sales stand as a dazzling scene, serving not just as a phase for high-stakes offering wars yet additionally as a pot where the destiny of establishments is reshaped each season. As we consider the effect of IPL Closeouts on the association, a diverse story arises, exemplifying the development, show, and vital complexities that have characterized this dynamic cricketing commercial center.

At its center, the IPL Sell-offs have re-imagined the actual texture of cricket by presenting a cutthroat player exchanging framework, wherein establishments bid for players to fabricate their crews without any preparation each season. This novel methodology cultivates a feeling of unusualness, infusing new energy into the association as groups go through critical changes many years. The closeouts have turned into an essential road for groups to recalibrate their methodologies, address shortcomings, and inject fresh blood into their line-ups.

The development of the IPL Closeouts reflects the more extensive change of T20 cricket into a super charged, diversion pressed design. Which began as a sober minded way to deal with collect serious groups inside monetary limitations has developed into a pompous occasion that orders worldwide consideration. The sales play rose above their practical part of player securing, arising as a marquee display that makes way for the cricketing event that continues in the association.

Decisively, the sales have turned into a chessboard where group proprietors, mentors, and research organizations participate in cerebral fights to get the right blend of players. The impact of examination, information driven bits of knowledge, and exploring networks has raised the dynamic interaction, with establishments utilizing a mix of cricketing insight and measurable accuracy to outmaneuver their opponents. The sales are not only about gaining headliners; they are tied in with building durable crews that can explore the special difficulties of T20 cricket.

A repetitive subject in the effect of IPL Sales is the production of a level battleground, disintegrating customary orders and giving more modest establishments potential chances to fight at a surprisingly high level. Not at all like long-design cricket, where authentic achievement frequently brings forth future predominance, T20 cricket's arrangement resets the condition each season. The barterings, through their populist nature, have empowered longshot groups to challenge the laid out request and arise as impressive competitors, adding a component of unusualness to the association.

The marquee players, the works of art of the sales, bring cricketing ability as well as turned into the substance of establishments, typifying the group's ethos and yearnings. The effect of marquee players reaches out past the limit ropes, impacting fan commitment, stock deals, and the general brand allure of the group. The sales, in this manner, act as a stage for obtaining ability as well as for building an establishment's character and fan following.

One of the nuanced effects of IPL Sell-offs lies in their job as an ability feature for arising players. Youthful cricketers, recently bound to homegrown circuits or lower-profile associations, have an opportunity to sling themselves into the spotlight through the closeouts. The IPL turns into a platform for their vocations, giving openness, experience, and the potential chance to hobnob with cricketing legends. The closeouts, in this sense, become a conductor for sustaining and uncovering cricketing ability, adding to the more extensive story of the association's job in molding what's to come stars of the game.

Monetary contemplations pose a potential threat in the effect of IPL Closeouts, as establishments explore the fragile harmony between marquee signings and financial plan requirements. The closeouts force groups to settle on canny monetary choices, guaranteeing that they secure effective players while remaining inside the bounds of pay covers. The monetary sharpness shown during the barterings is a demonstration of an establishment's maintainability and capacity to work in a cutthroat cricketing economy.

The effect of IPL Closeouts stretches out a long ways past the cricketing clique, reverberating with a worldwide crowd and drawing in fans in an all year cricketing cycle. The expectation and furor paving the way to the barterings, the happiness of getting valued players, and the essential discussions that follow add to the vivid experience for fans. The sales, in this manner, become a urgent component in the association's capacity to spellbind and hold the consideration of cricket lovers all over the planet.

Be that as it may, in the midst of the charm and fabulousness, the effect of IPL Sell-offs isn't without any trace of difficulties and reactions. The slanted spotlight on laid out stars some of the time eclipses the capability of unheralded gifts, prompting worries about the disregard of homegrown players. The tireless quest for marquee names, on occasion, brings about swelled costs, bringing up issues about the monetary practicality of such speculations and the drawn out maintainability of establishments.

The effect of IPL Closeouts in group elements and brotherhood can't be neglected. While the barterings give a chance to produce winning blends, the successive reshuffling of groups difficulties the advancement of stable group societies. Building trust, grasping playing styles, and cultivating a feeling of solidarity become continuous difficulties for establishments, impacting their capacity to perform reliably on the field.

The sale elements additionally feature the more extensive monetary powers at play in the cricketing scene. The association's capacity to draw in strong sponsorship bargains, broadcast freedoms, and worldwide crowds is unpredictably attached to the achievement and allure of the closeouts. The effect of IPL Sales, consequently, stretches out past the wearing field, molding the monetary environment of present day cricket and setting benchmarks for different associations trying to imitate its prosperity.

As the IPL Sales keep on developing, their effect on cricket's scene is ready to extend. The association remains at the crossing point of custom and advancement, utilizing the ageless allure of cricket while embracing the dynamism of the T20 design. The sales, with their mix of show, procedure, and worldwide star power, have turned into a microcosm of the steadily developing cricketing story, leaving a permanent engraving on the game's present and future.

9.6 Looking ahead to the future of IPL Auctions and team strategies

As the Indian Chief Association (IPL) keeps on spellbinding cricket devotees around the world, the fate of IPL Closeouts and group procedures holds fascinating conceivable outcomes that guarantee to reshape the scene of T20 cricket. Looking forward, a few vital patterns and potential improvements offer a brief look into what the future might hold for the closeouts and the groups competing for matchless quality in the association.

One of the first contemplations for the eventual fate of IPL Closeouts is the continuous journey for a sensitive harmony between star power and group union. While marquee players bring their singular brightness, establishments progressively perceive the significance of developing an amicable group culture. Looking forward, groups could put an uplifted accentuation on distinguishing players who have extraordinary cricketing abilities as well as contribute decidedly to the group elements, encouraging a feeling of solidarity and mutual perspective.

The impact of information examination and innovation is ready to turn out to be much more articulated in forming group systems during the barterings. With a consistently growing pool of players and a wealth of execution measurements accessible, establishments are probably going to put vigorously in cutting edge examination to acquire an upper hand. Prescient demonstrating, player profiling, and vital experiences got from information could assume a critical part in directing sale choices, assisting groups with recognizing underestimated players and art balanced crews.

The idea of player maintenance and coherence is supposed to acquire unmistakable quality later on scene of IPL Sell-offs. Groups perceiving the benefit of holding center players, who exemplify the establishment's personality and playing style, may select long haul affiliations. This shift could prompt a more steady player base, empowering groups to expand on existing blends, improve group science, and cultivate a more profound association among players and fans over progressive seasons.

The developing job of uncapped players in group methodologies is one more viewpoint to watch in ongoing sell-offs. While marquee signings snatch titles, uncapped players frequently arise as unexpected, yet invaluable treasures, giving great profits from venture. Establishments could progressively zero in on exploring and supporting neighborhood gifts, perceiving the capability of unheralded players to make significant commitments. What's to come closeouts could observer a more deliberate work to uncover and grandstand the gifts of arising cricketers.

As far as spending plan contemplations, establishments are probably going to refine their systems to explore the complexities of compensation covers and monetary imperatives. With the association's monetary scene developing, groups might take on inventive ways to deal with expand the effect of their spending. Vital spending plan portion, prudent offering, and a keen comprehension of player values could turn out to be much more basic as establishments try to construct serious crews while sticking to monetary reasonability.

The worldwide kind of the IPL is supposed to endure, with establishments proceeding to scout and get abroad players who bring assorted abilities and encounters. Nonetheless, there could be a change in the assessment rules, with groups putting more noteworthy accentuation on players who adjust flawlessly to the difficulties of Indian circumstances. Adaptability in assuming various parts, adjusting to various organizations, and flourishing under tension in subcontinental conditions might become key contemplations for abroad signings.

The idea of dynamic group building, wherein establishments tailor their techniques to suit the particular requests of each season, is probably going to get some decent forward momentum. Groups could embrace a more adaptable and versatile methodology, perceiving that the necessities for progress can differ from one season to another. This could prompt a more iterative and vital development of groups, with each closeout cycle filling in as a chance for recalibration in light of the learnings from the first season.

Establishment proprietors and the executives are supposed to assume an undeniably essential part in forming group systems during the barterings. Past monetary support, proprietors might turn out to be more engaged with cricketing choices, bringing a mix of business keenness and cricketing understanding to the table. The arrangement between proprietorship vision and on-field procedures could turn into an unequivocal figure an establishment's capacity to support achievement and construct an enduring heritage in the IPL.

The fate of IPL Sales could likewise observe developments in the bartering design itself. The association coordinators could investigate ways of improving the show and exhibition, keeping fans connected all through the closeout interaction. Presenting new offering components, intuitive fan association, or integrating innovation to give constant bits of knowledge into group independent direction could be not too far off, adding layers of fervor to the sales.

As the association keeps on extending its impression universally, the job of IPL Sell-offs in molding global cricketing accounts is set to develop. The closeouts act as a stage for players from different cricketing countries to exhibit their abilities, adding to the globalization of T20 cricket. The future could observer a considerably more different pool of worldwide players partaking in the IPL, further lifting the association's status as a blend of cricketing ability.